IRON SPOKESHAVES AND RELATED TOOLS MANUFACTURED BY EDWARD PRESTON & SONS

Joe Stankus

Research assistance by Ron Peel and Chris Ellis

Copyright © 2020 by Joe Stankus

Research assistance by Ron Peel and Chris Ellis

All rights reserved. No part of this book may be reproduced in any form or by any electrical or mechanical means, including photocopying, information storage and/or retrieval systems, without permission in writing from the author.

First Edition

ISBN 978-1-7350042-0-4 hardcover
ISBN 978-1-7350042-1-1 paperback

Unless otherwise noted, all photographs by Joe Stankus

The excerpts and illustrations from historical documents, including, but not limited to patent abridgements, patent specifications, advertisements, catalogue entries, and announcements that are included in this work are believed to be in the public domain.

Cover by Tony Stankus

Produced and Published by Joe Stankus

Joe Stankus
217 Haciendas Dr
Weatherford, Texas 76087
Joe_2718@yahoo.com

Acknowledgements

My gratitude is extended to many individuals who have assisted and supported in my efforts in this project.

I am especially grateful to Chris Ellis and Jane Rees who graciously shared information from their catalogue collections and research.

I would also like to recognize the significant contributions of Ron Peel. Ron has graciously shared his knowledge of patternmaking, his collection of Preston spokeshaves, and has done research for this treatise at the Birmingham Central Library.

Contributors

John Eaton
Chris Ellis
Ken Hawley Charitable Trust
Tom Lamond
Drew Lamond
Patrick Leach
Rob Lee
Ron Peel
Jane Rees
John Stankus

Special Appreciation

I am especially grateful for the support and encouragement of my wife, Tali, our children Rachel, Matt, and Kaylee, and our granddaughter Avery. Additionally, Rachel has been proudly promoting this book far in advance of is publication. I would also like to thank my parents, Pat and Jack, and my brothers, John and Tony, for their assistance and input. I am thankful that my friends and family did not consider me an eccentric as I amassed an extensive collection of spokeshaves (a tool which most of the population has never seen) from a company that ceased trading over 80 years ago.

A Note From Rachel

Rachel and Matt seeking treasures at a tool swap meet in 2008. Photograph courtesy of Jim Goodson.

Dad,

I am so happy that you are able to write this book. It brings back such great memories of hanging out in the workshop drinking root beer and eating chocolate while trying to solder those light up kits, when in all honesty, we were just soldering them to your workbench. I hope these spokeshaves stay as our reminder of those great times. Thank you for teaching me your skills with woodworking and thank you for being the best dad with the coolest spokeshaves.

Your Woodworking Buddy, your daughter,

Rachel

Table of Contents

A Brief history of Preston 1
Patents assigned to Edward Preston for Spokeshave and Related Tools 4
    British Patents 4
    Patent 13,713 4
    Patent 12,458 5
    Patent 8,291 6
    Patent 1,667 7
    Patent 15,549 8
    Patent 17,234 9
    Patent 20,062 10
    Patent 13,699 11
    Patent 20,216 12
British Design Patents 13
    181,531 1891 Lightweight stringing router 13
    322,021   July 15, 1898   Spokeshave Design 14
    328,028   Oct. 25, 1898   Router Design 15
    356,049   Apr. 12, 1900   Spokeshave Design 16
The Evolution of the Preston Adjustable Spokeshave 17
Tools Manufactured for the Trade 19
76 Iron Spokeshave 21
77 Iron Spokeshave 22
78 Iron Spokeshave 23
79 Iron Spokeshave 24
80 Iron Spokeshave 25
81 Iron Spokeshave 26
82 Adjustable Mouth Iron Spokeshave 27
83 Iron Spokeshave 28
87 Iron Spokeshave 29
88 Iron Spokeshave 30
89 Iron Chamfer Spokeshave 31
180 Cabinet Scraper 32
1373 Registered Iron Spokeshave 33

1374 Registered Iron Spokeshave ... 34
1374P Registered Iron Spokeshave ... 35
1377 Patent Iron Spokeshave ... 37
Unidentified Early Preston Iron Spokeshave ... 40
1379 Iron Spokeshave ... 41
1380 Iron Spokeshave ... 42
1380 ½ Iron Spokeshave ... 43
1381 Iron Spokeshave ... 44
1381 ½ Iron Spokeshave ... 45
1382 Iron Spokeshave ... 47
1382 ½ Iron Spokeshave ... 48
1383 Iron Spokeshave ... 49
1383 ½ Iron Spokeshave ... 50
1384 Iron Spokeshave ... 51
1385 Improved Chamfer Shave ... 52
1386 Improved Circular Rabbeting and Fillister Router ... 53
1387A Improved Circular Sash Router–Oveloe ... 54
1387B Improved Circular Sash Router – Lamb Tongue ... 57
1387C Improved Circular Sash Router– Gothic ... 59
1387D Improved Circular Common Oveloe Router ... 61
1387E Improved Circular Equal or Square Oveloe Router ... 62
1388 Improved Circular Quirk or Grooving Router ... 64
1388P Patent Adjustable Circular Quirk or Grooving Router ... 66
1389 Improved Circular Bead Router ... 68
1390 Patent Iron Spokeshave ... 71
1390H Patent Iron Spokeshave ... 73
1391 Patent Iron Spokeshave ... 79
1392 Patent Adjustable Stop Chamfer Shave ... 81
1393 Patent Hand Reeder and Moulding Tool ... 84
1393P Patent Adjustable Hand Reeder and Moulding Tool ... 86
1393S Patent Reeding, Rabbeting, and Moulding tool ... 88
1394 Patent Adjustable Circular Quirk or Grooving Router ... 90
1395 Patent Adjustable Circular Quirk or Grooving Router ... 92

1396 Preston Patent Lining or Stringing Router 94

1396F Preston Patent Lining or Stringing Router with removable faceplate 97

1398 Preston Patent Lining or Stringing Router with round adjustable sliding rod and removable pointed screw pin 99

2501 Spokeshave with offset handles 100

2502 Patent Iron Spokeshave 101

2503 Patent Iron Spokeshave 102

2504 Patent Adjustable Twin Handle, Malleable Iron Rabbeting Shave 104

Charles Parkin & Son's Registered Hand Beader 105

Checklist 107

Listing of Catalogues and Other Ephemera 113

References 115

Introduction

My interest in Preston spokeshaves started when I read Thomas Lamond's book, *Manufactured and Patented Spokeshaves & Similar Tools*. I purchased my first Preston spokeshave from Jim Bode and was amazed by how well it worked. I started acquiring more Preston spokeshaves and I decided to display them at the SWTCA Yukon meet in January 2011. I started compiling the information for the display and decided that it would be very useful to have a checklist of all the spokeshaves, related tools, and all of the variations. This reference is the result.

One of the most rewarding outcomes of researching and writing this reference was meeting fellow collectors and making new friends. Tom Lamond was very helpful in the beginning of this project. When Tom passed away, I exchanged a lot of emails with Drew Lamond, Tom's son. Drew gave me all of his father's research on Preston spokeshaves. I also met Chris Ellis, who had accumulated a large collection of trade catalogues. Most of the original Preston, Melhuish, and Nurse catalogues referenced in the production of this treatise are from his collection. Chris introduced me to Ron Peel. Ron is a Preston collector. Ron has been to the Birmingham Public Library on many occasions to help with research needed to make this treatise possible. Over the years, we have shared a lot of information, theories, and conjectures about Preston. The quality of this treatise was greatly enhanced by the contributions made by Ron Peel and Chris Ellis. I greatly appreciate their assistance and friendship.

Joe Stankus

February 2020

A Brief History of Preston

Edward Preston & Sons Ltd. traces its roots back to June 1825, when Edward Preston Senior started making planes at 77 Lichfield Street, Birmingham. Edward Preston Sr. expanded his business and was listed as a planemaker, manufacturer of joiner's tools, and general dealer of Sheffield tools of all descriptions doing business in the 1849 Birmingham directory. In 1855, No. 77 Lichfield Street had been renumbered to 97 Lichfield Street. The 1876 Birmingham Directory listed Henry Preston, Edward Preston Jr.'s younger brother, as son and successor to Edward Preston at 97 Lichfield Street. Henry Preston's 1875 price list does not contain any iron spokeshaves nor does the 1876 Birmingham business directory include spokeshaves in the list of products made by Henry Preston. This would indicate that Preston spokeshave manufacturing was most likely introduced by Edward Preston Jr.

By 1864, Edward Preston Junior had established his own business at 97 ½ Lichfield Street. He moved his operations to 26 Newton Street in 1868, and then finally in 1874 to 22-24 Whittall Street. In 1903, a new factory was designed and built to new methods of manufacturing and to provide additional space. Edward Preston would remain at Whittall Street until the business ceased trading.

It is most likely that iron spokeshaves were first produced by Preston after 1875 and before 1879. An 1876 advertisement does not mention spokeshaves, but two spokeshaves are illustrated in an 1879 advertisement.

Advertisement from the 1876 *Birmingham Business Directory*

Advertisement from the *Australian and New Zealand Gazette,* March 15, 1879

An advertisement in the March 15, 1879 *Australian and New Zealand Gazette* shows illustrations of the 1384 and 1385 spokeshaves. There are also references to iron spokeshaves made by Edward Preston in the 1879 Sidney Exhibition.

Advertisement from *The British Trade Journal,* October 1, 1880.

The advertisement in the October 1, 1880 edition of *The British Trade Journal* indicates that Edward Preston manufactures iron spokeshaves, sash routers, and rabbeting routers. The illustration in the advertisement appears to be a model 1379 spokeshave. The Preston rabbeting router is the model 1386. Preston sash routers are models 1387A, 1387B, and 1387C.

The 1379, 1380, 1381, 1382, and 1383 spokeshaves appear to be copies of spokeshaves that were invented by Leonard Bailey and are commonly known as Boston Bailey spokeshaves. Bailey had United States patent number 21311, issued August 3, 1858, that covered the blade clamping mechanism of the 1381 and 1381 ½. He also had United States patent 20855, issued July 13, 1858, that covered the adjustable mouth of the 1382 and 1382 ½. The Bailey patents expired in 1875, further adding to circumstantial evidence that Preston spokeshaves were introduced after 1875.

The sash routers, rabbeting router, and quirk router are of decidedly British origin as they were only offered by British toolmakers. There is no information that indicates who introduced these tools. Additionally, as these sashmaking tools and quirk routers were not patented, it is unclear whether they were made exclusively by Preston and distributed by other manufacturers, or if these tools were made by several manufacturers using similar patterns.

Henry Preston's business failed in 1882 and a creditor's meeting was held on October 16th of that year. The bankruptcy notice indicated that this was liquidation by arrangement or composition with creditors. It is likely that Edward Preston acquired some or all of Henry's business assets in this proceeding.

The Preston Patent adjuster was patented on October 19, 1885. The patent illustrations show the adjustment mechanism on a 1392 chamfer shave which was announced in the January 1, 1886 edition of *The British Trade Journal*. The Preston Patent Adjuster would eventually be seen on many planes and spokeshaves. No other tools were mentioned in this announcement.

Edward Preston Jr. made his three sons partners in the business in 1889. This resulted in changing the firm's name to Edward Preston & Sons. In 1898, the business was converted into a limited company, which further changed the name to Edward Preston & Sons, Ltd.

Edward Preston acquired Registered Design status for the 1391 in 1898 and for the 1373 and 1374 spokeshaves in 1900. This registered design covered the highly recognizable embellishment that was cast into these spokeshaves. Preston had also received a registered design number for adding the same embellishment to sash routers, but never put it into production.

At some point, Preston renumbered some of their spokeshaves and introduced spokeshaves that seemed to be copies of Stanley designs. As no Preston catalogues after 1914 and prior to 1932 are available to the author, it is not possible to accurately state when these changes were implemented, but it seems most likely that this occurred in the 1920s. The Richard Melhuish Catalogue No. 25, published in 1925, shows the designs that were available in the 1909 Edward Preston catalogue and the new model 80 spokeshave. It is likely that other models in the 76 through 89 range were introduced around this time. The 1379, 1380, 1381, 1382, and 1383 models were probably discontinued with the introduction of the 78, 79, 80, 81, and 82. The model 87 spokeshave, which was a copy of the Stanley 151 with a round face, was not in the 1932 Preston catalogue, but was in the 1933 Rabone catalogue, which would indicate a late 1932 or early 1933 introduction.

Edward Preston and Sons Ltd had fallen into financial difficulties in the early 1930s and was sold to John Rabone and Sons in October 1932. The iron department, which included plane and spokeshave manufacturing continued under Rabone. The 1933 Rabone catalogue listed 11 Preston spokeshaves and related tools. The plane and spokeshave business was not performing satisfactorily and on October 10, 1934, C & J Hampton had taken over the manufacturing rights to hand planes, spokeshaves, brass plumb bobs and beech mitre boxes.

Patents assigned to Edward Preston for Spokeshave and Related Tools

British Patents

Before 1916 British patent numbers returned to one at the beginning of each year. In 1916 a continuous number series began, starting with 100001. From 1884 to 1915 British patent numbers were assigned very early in the application process. Many were never published because the application was rejected or the applicant gave up early in the process.

A patent specification contains a full description of the invention, plus any drawings referred to within the description, as well as one or more claims. A claim is a precise statement of the innovation that is protected. The first claim must define the invention by specifying its distinctive technical features. These are the features which distinguish the invention from what is already known within the same or similar field.

A patent abridgement gives a concise description of the invention together with the inventor's name, the patent title and date. In the United Kingdom, there are two sets of abridgments which cover the period 1617-1890. Patents after 1890 can be searched in Espacenet, a free online patent search tool.

Patent 13,713

Title: **Spokeshaves**
Date of Application: 1884
Inventor: Edward Preston

This patent application was abandoned and superseded by patent 12,458.

Patent 12,458

Title: **Improvements in Spoke-shaves, Planes, and other similar Tools**
Date of Application: Oct. 19, 1885
Inventor: Edward Preston

This patent covers "Preston's Patent depth adjuster".

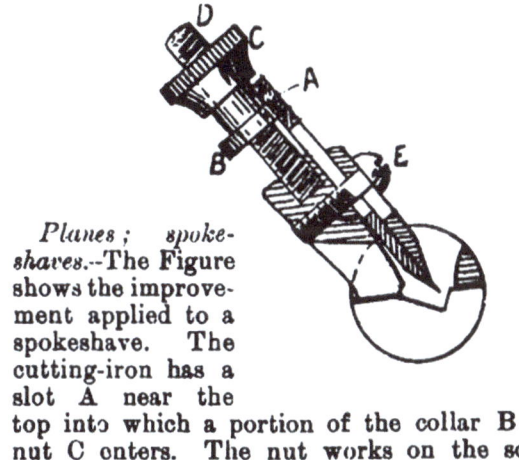

12,458. Preston, E. Oct. 19.

Planes; spoke-shaves.--The Figure shows the improvement applied to a spokeshave. The cutting-iron has a slot A near the top into which a portion of the collar B on the nut C enters. The nut works on the screw D attached to the body of the plane. When the set-screw E is loose, the cutting-iron can be set in any position by the nut. The irons are clamped together and to the body of the plane by the set-screw.

Patent 12,458 Abridgement

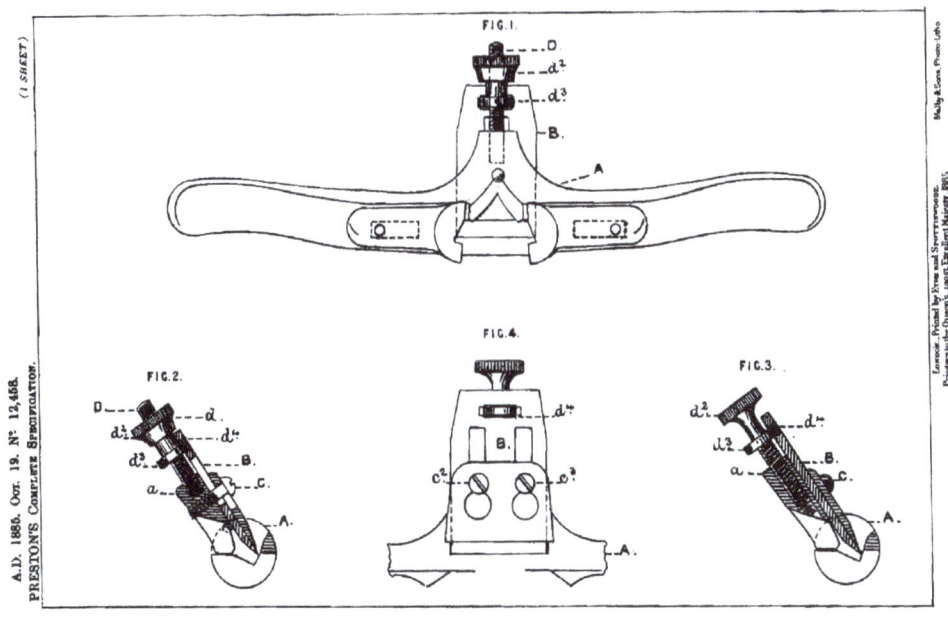

Patent 12,458 diagram

Patent 8,291

Title: **Spokeshaves**
Date of Application: June 23, 1886
Inventor: Edward Preston

This patent covers the hand reeder blade clamp as seen on the 1393.

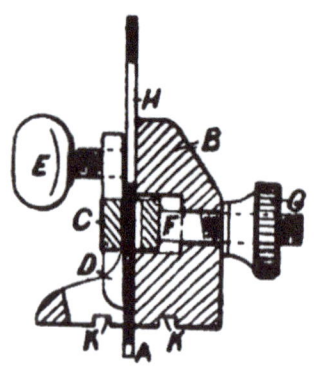

8291. Preston, E. June 23.

Planes; spokeshaves.—Relates to routers for quirking &c. The Figure shows a transverse section of the tool, which is operated after the manner of a spokeshave. The cutting-iron A is held against the bed B by the long slotted bar C, formed with the plate D carrying the thumb-screw E, and with the bolt F for the milled nut G. The thumb-screw passes through the slot H in the cutting-iron and bears against the bed B so as to firmly clamp the cutting-iron near its edge. The fence has ribs to fit into the grooves K in the face, and a slot so that it may slide over and mask part of the cutting-edge, which may be shaped for beading, reeding, or quirking.

Patent 8,291 Abridgement

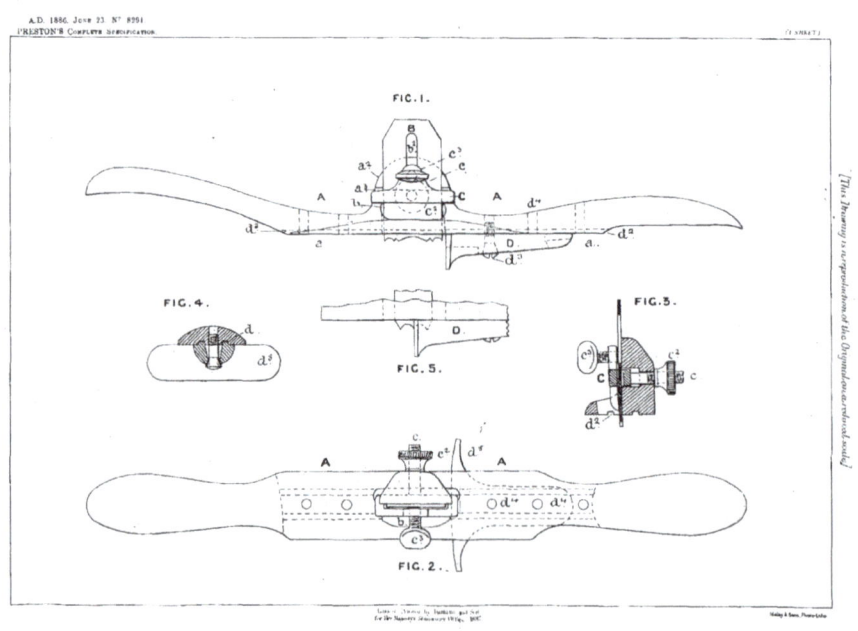

Patent 8,291 diagram

Patent 1,667

Title: Routers
Date of Application: Feb. 4, 1888
Inventor: Edward Preston

This patent covers the small moulding tool model 1393S.

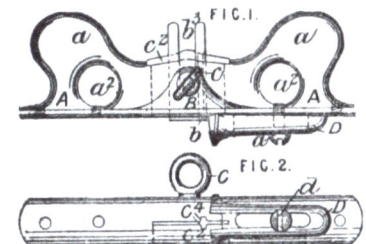

1667. Preston, E. Feb. 4.

Routers.—Relates to improvements in "routers" for adapting them for rabbeting, grooving, and moulding the margins of circular, oval, &c. openings in brackets, frames, &c. to receive mirrors, pictures, and the like ; and for grooving, for inlaying, and for bevelling the outer margins of various articles. Various kinds of work may be done by this tool ; rabbeting may be done by first cutting a groove with the small cutter and then using the wide cutter. Fig. 1 shows an elevation of the tool, and Fig. 2 an underside view. The frame A, about four or five inches long, is formed with lugs a, and openings a^2 for the fingers and thumbs instead of the usual handles. The tool cutter is clamped between the bracket B, preferably formed in one casting with the frame and the back plate c^2 by the thumb-screw c. Two forms of cutters may be used, namely, the wide cutter b formed with a slot b^3 to enable it to be removed without taking out the thumb-screw c; and, secondly, a narrow cutter which is held in the vertical cross-slots c^4 in the frame and back plate respectively. The fence D is like that described in Specification No. 8291, A.D. 1886, being adjusted by a screw d and grooved beneath to mask part of the cutter.

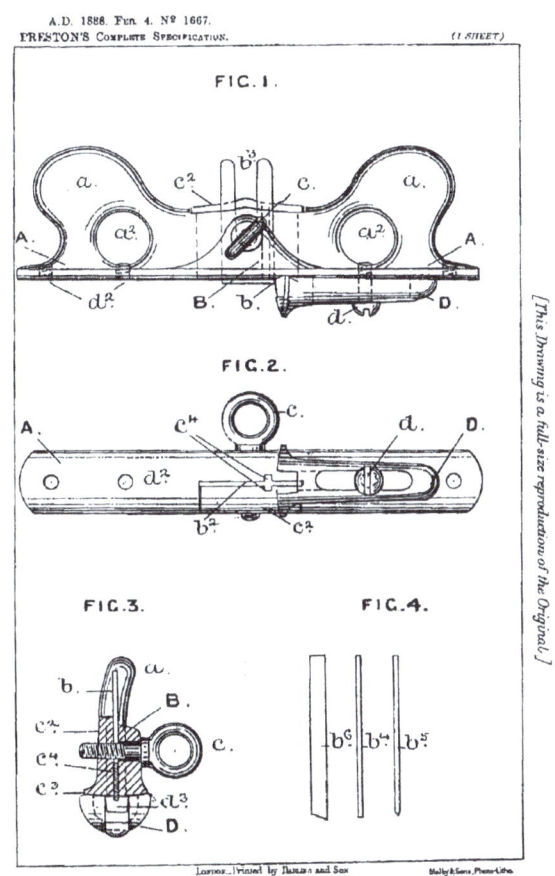

Patent 1,667 Abridgement

Patent 1,667 Diagram

Patent 15,549

Title: **Improvements in Spoke-shaves and other similar Tools**
Date of Application: July 15, 1898
Complete Specification Left: February 25, 1899
Accepted: April 1, 1899
Inventor: Edward Preston

This patent covers the shape of the notch in the cutting iron.

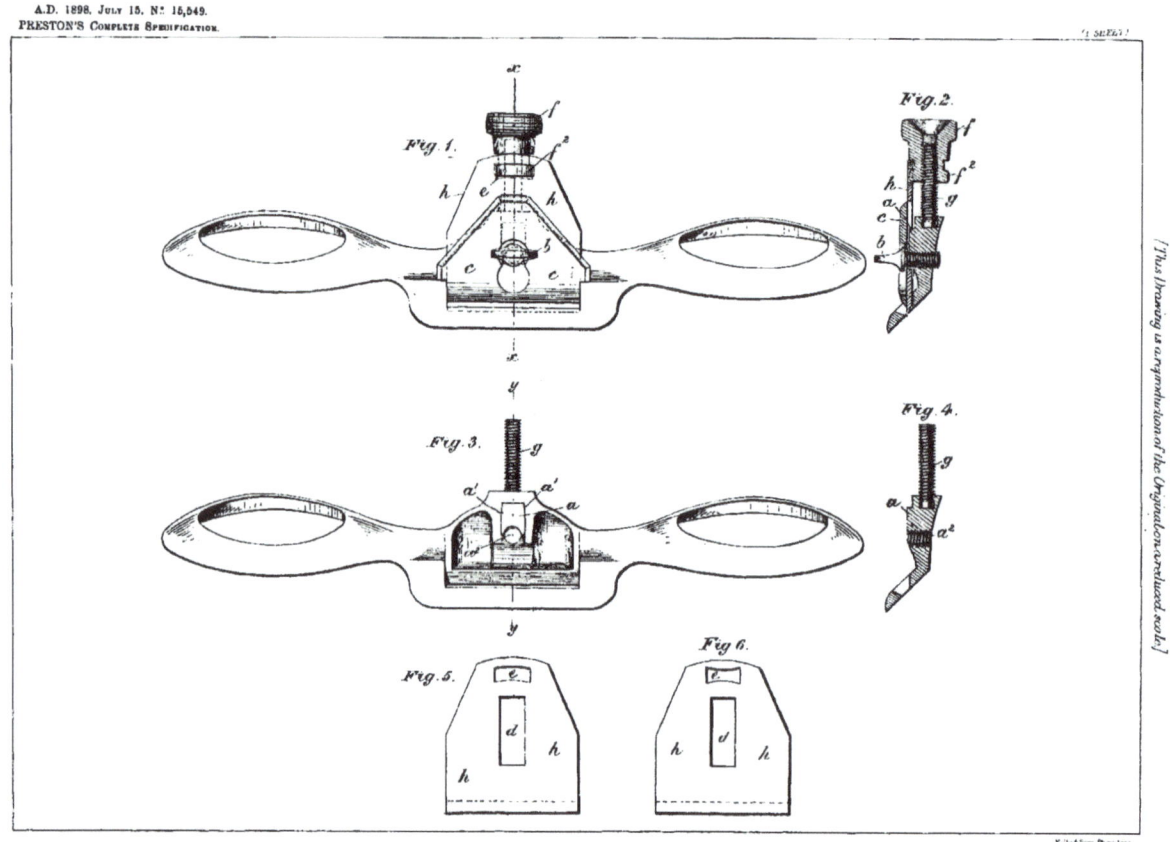

Patent 15,549 diagram

The slot in the cutting-iron , and the projection a for the slot d, are curved so that, besides the longitudinal adjustment of the cutter effected by the nut, the cutter may be tilted slightly in a lateral direction to bring its edge parallel to the slot through which it projects.

Patent 17,234

Title: **Improvements in Spoke-shaves and other similar Tools**
Date of Application: August 17, 1908
Inventor: Edward Preston

This patent covers adjustable handles that were not seen in any tools produced by Preston.

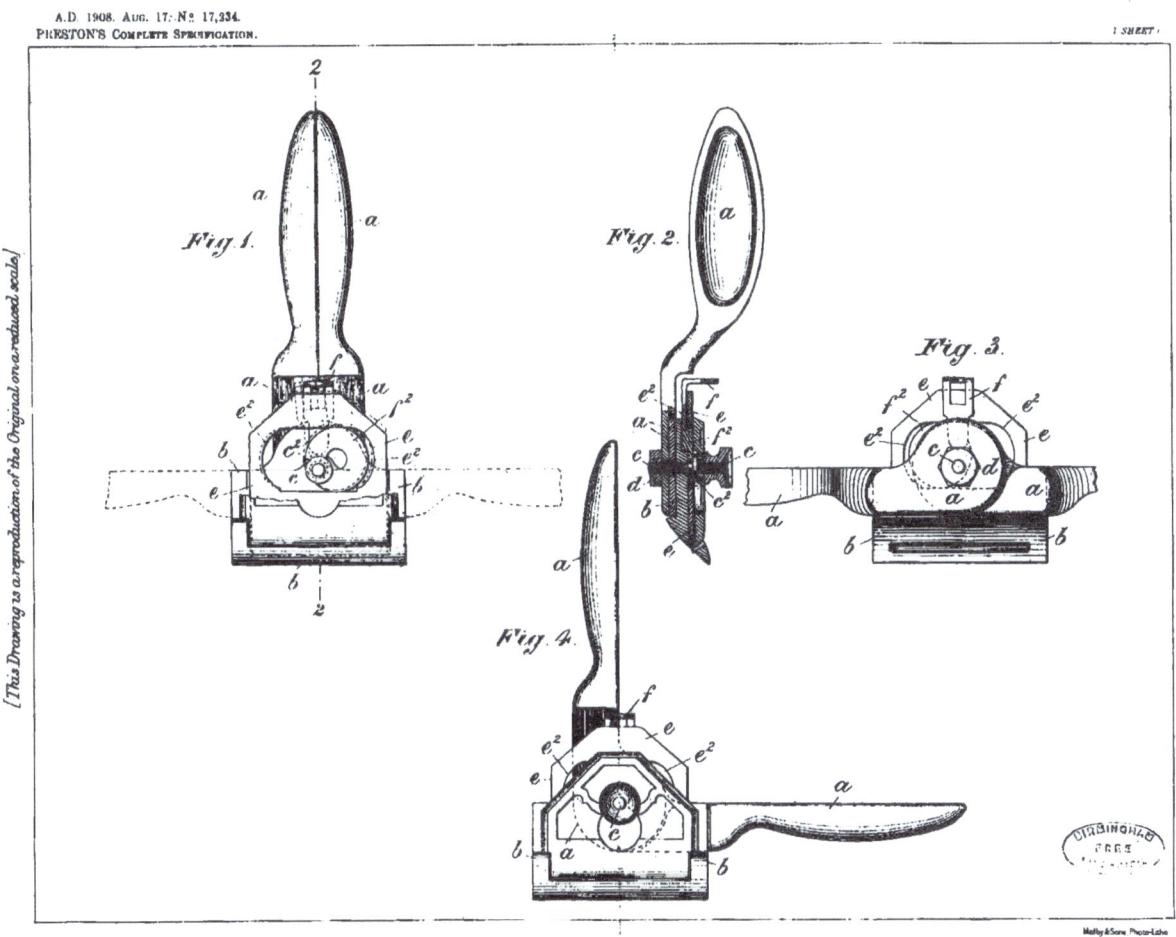

Patent 17,234 diagram

In spokeshaves and like tools the arms or handles are made separate from the body and are pivoted to it by a bolt, so that the position of the handles relatively to the body may be adjusted. Means are provided for longitudinally adjusting the cutting-iron consisting of a lever, pivoted on a collar on the bolt and having a cam-shaped part, which engages a cross-slot in the cutting-iron.

Patent 20,062

Title: **Improvements in Spoke-shaves and other similar Tools**
Date of Application: September 24, 1908
Inventor: Edward Preston

This patent covers a blade adjustment mechanism that did not go into production

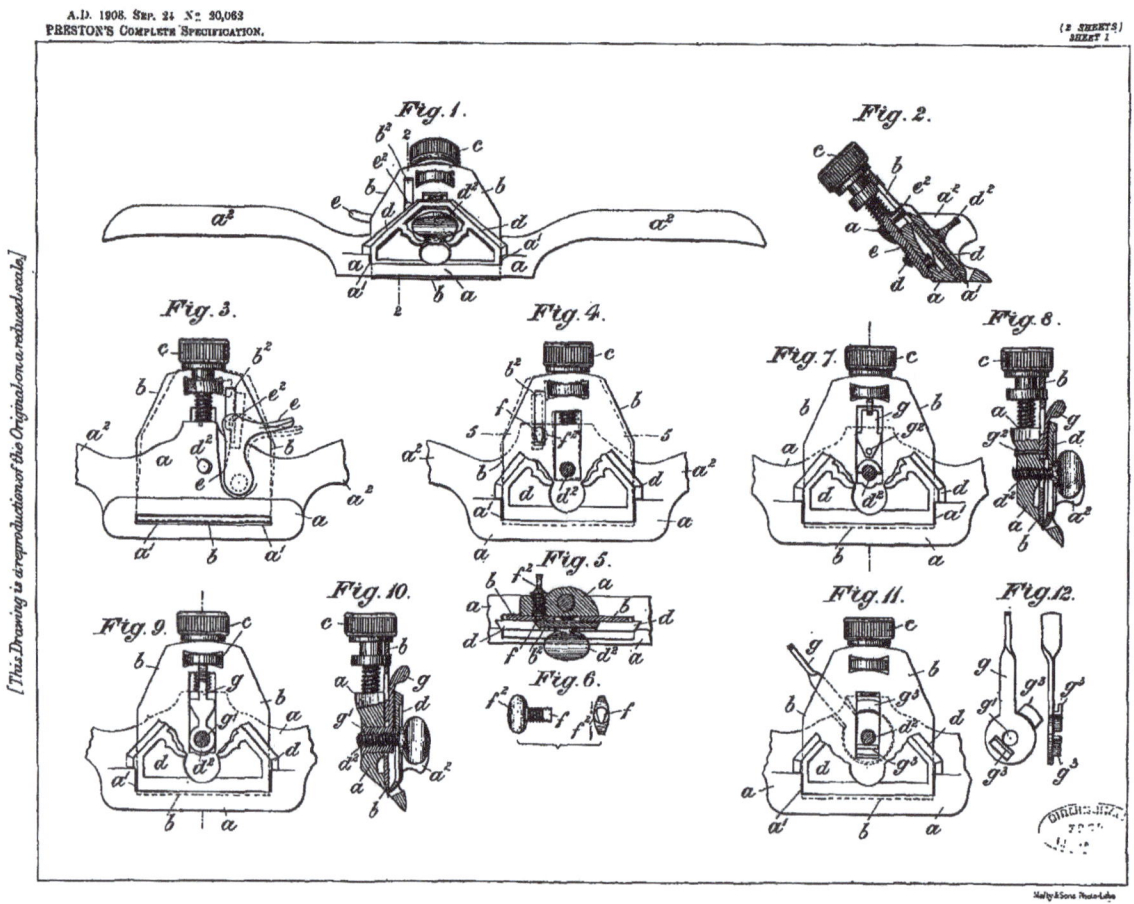

Patent 20,062 diagram

Spokeshaves and like tools of the type described in Specifications No. 12,458, A.D. 1885, and No. 15,549, A.D. 1898, are provided with mechanical means for laterally adjusting the cutting-iron. A bell-crank lever is pivoted to the body, and is provided with a pin which engages with a longitudinal slot in the cutting-iron. Various modifications are described in which the adjustment is effected by rocking-levers of various shapes, or by a cam on the end of a screw engaging a longitudinal slot. The invention may be applied to planes.

Patent 13,699

Title: **Improvements in Spoke-shaves and other similar Tools**
Date of Application: 1911
Inventor: Edward Preston

This patent covers a fence adjustment system that was not seen in any tools produced by Preston.

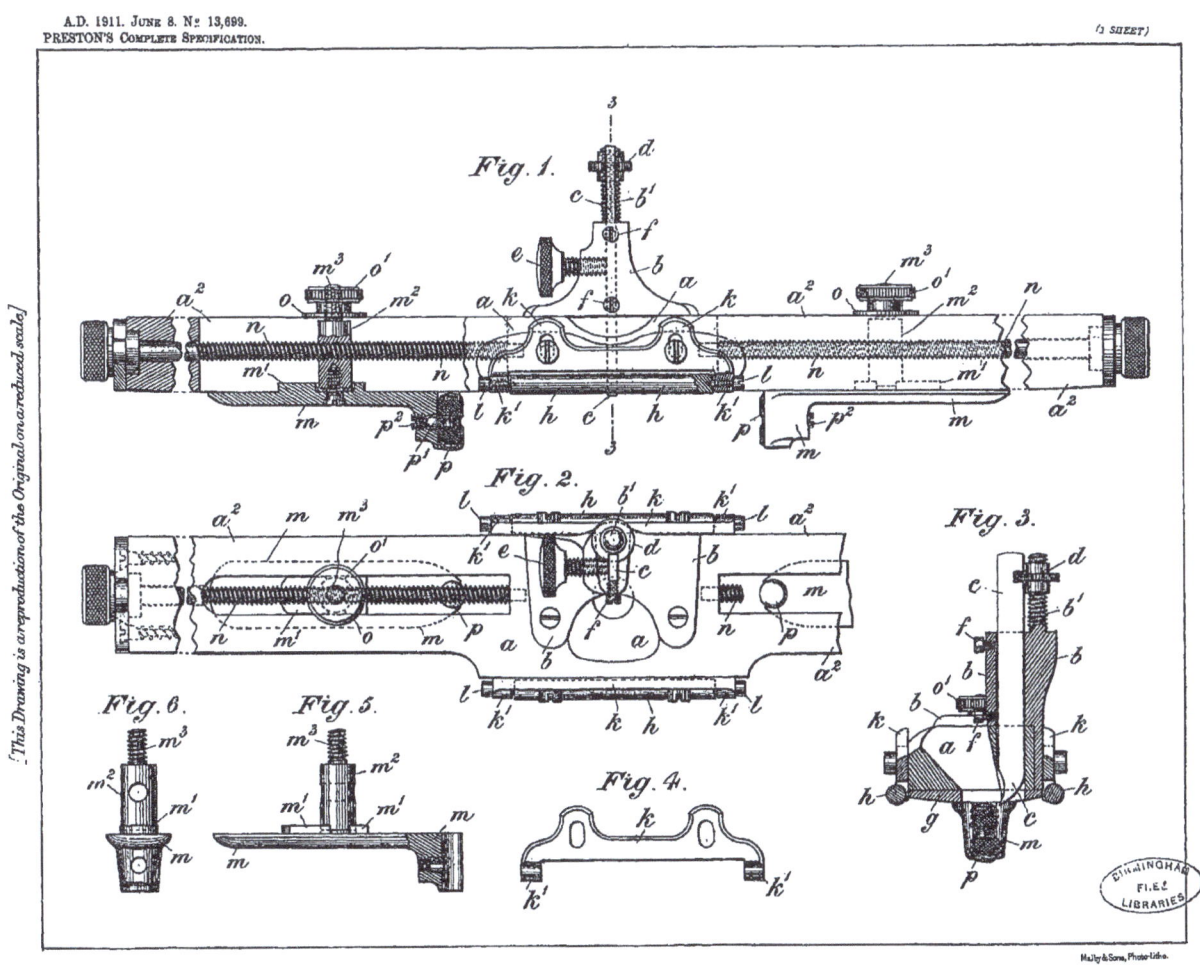

Patent 13,699 diagram

Spokeshaves and like tools, such as are described in Specifications 12,458/85, 15,549/98, and 20,062/08, are provided with an axial screw n in each handle which threads through a vertical post m^2 on the adjustable fence m. The vertical posts m^2 work in slots in the handles, and are locked in position by a nut o^1 screwing on to the threaded end of the post. The fences are provided with anti-friction rollers p mounted in sockets open on the acting face of the fence and held in place by balls p^1 engaging grooves in the rollers. Rollers h, carried in adjustable frames k, are mounted at the front and back edges of the face-plate. The tool may be fixed after adjustment by a side screw e and two setscrews f bearing against the vertical edge of the tool.

Patent 20,216

Title: **Improvements in or relating to Spoke-shaves or like Hand Tools**
Date of Application: 1912
Inventor: Edward Preston and C.E Saunders

This patent covers the blade adjustment mechanism as found in model 2502 and 2503 spokeshaves

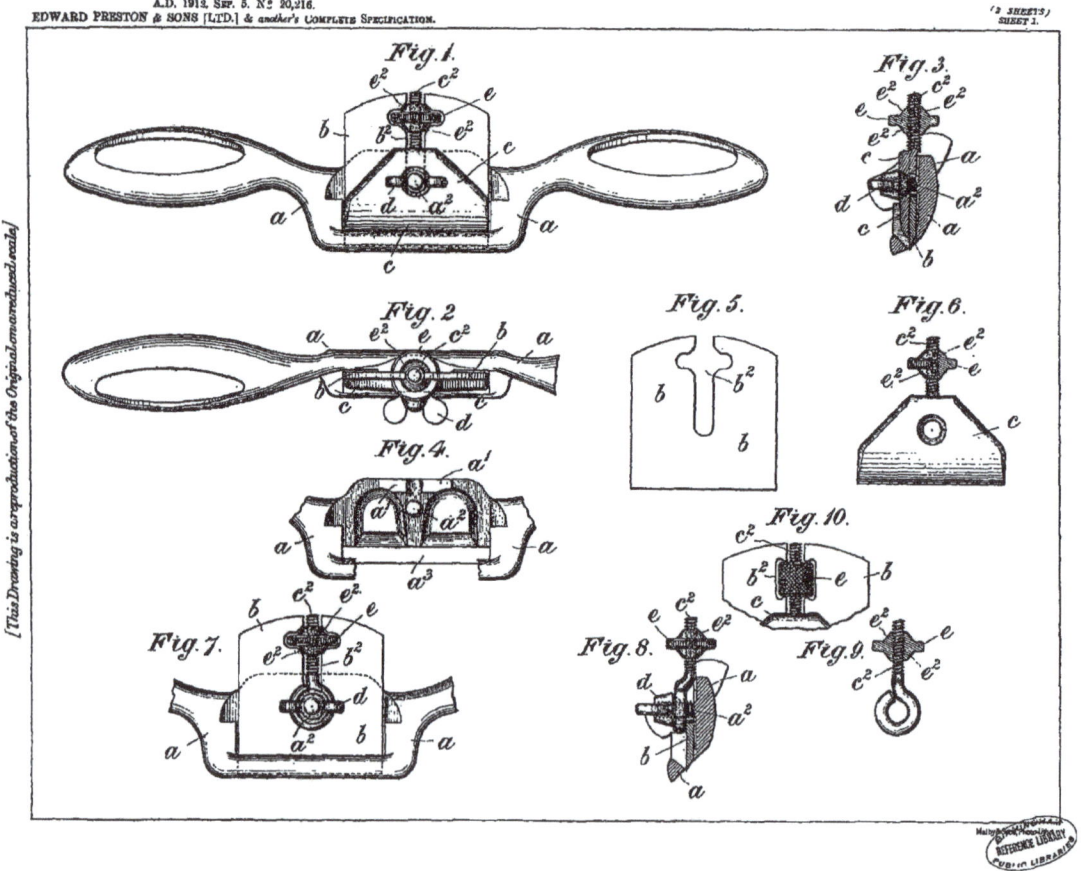

Patent 20,216 diagram

Planes, spokeshaves, and like tools of the kind in which the cutting-iron is adjusted by means of a stationary screw and a nut thereon engaging with a slot in the cutting-iron have the parts so arranged that the axis of the screw is in the same plane as the cutting-iron. The adjusting-screw c^2 is preferably made integral with the cover-plate c and is accommodated in the longitudinal slot b^2 in the cutting-iron b, this slot having transverse extensions to receive the adjusting-nut e formed with conical bearing- bosses e^2. The adjusting-screw may be separate from the cover-plate and formed with two projecting pins or a single key taking into holes or a slot therein; or, as shown in Fig. 8, it may be formed with a cranked eye, in which case the cover-plate may be dispensed with. The clamping-nut d on the screw-post a^2 is preferably formed with a conical end fitting into a countersunk hole in the cover-plate or screw-eye, as shown in Figs. 3 and 8. In the plane shown in Fig. 11 the adjusting-screw c^2 has a cross-pin c^1 engaging a hole or groove f in the body a and is grooved longitudinally to receive the edges of the slot in the cutting-iron.

British Design Patents

181,531 1891 Lightweight stringing router

Design: Registered Hand Beader
Registered by: Charles Parkin and Son

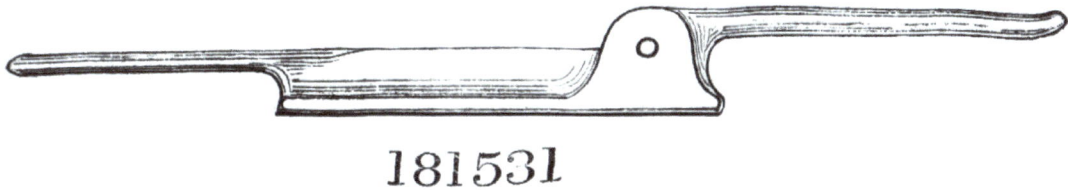

BT 50/165 Designs 165 Designs 181152-182087 1891182087 1891 Oct. 20 – Nov. 2

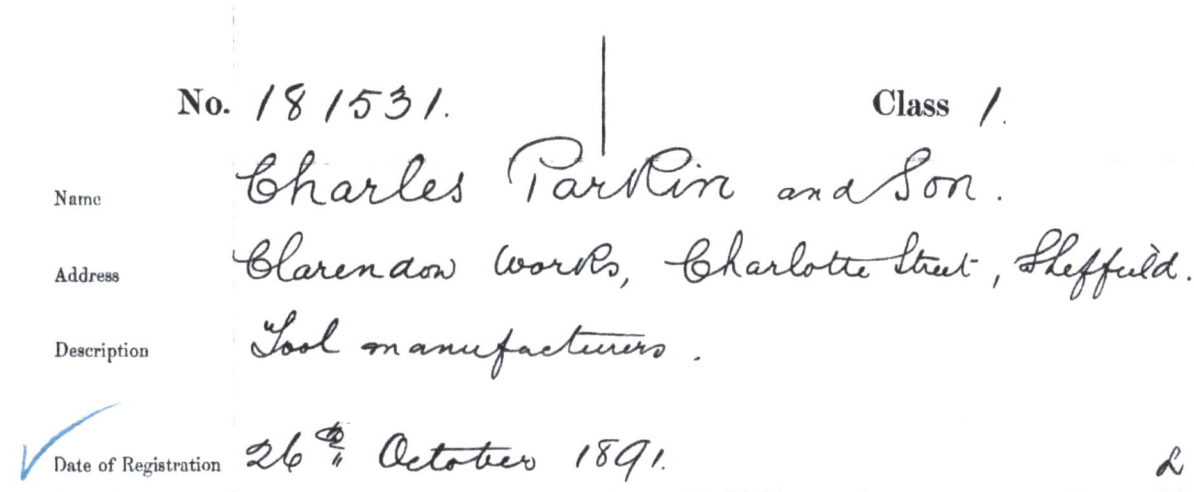

BT 51/66 Designs 180829-185824 1891 Oct. 14 - 1892 Jan. 5

The lightweight stringing router is generally attributed to Preston; however the registered design indicates that the lightweight stringing router was actually a product of Charles Parkin and Son, Clarendon Works, Charlotte Street, Sheffield. Additionally, this router was never listed in any Preston catalogue available to the author but was listed in the 1892 and 1899 Richard Melhuish catalogues.

322,021   July 15, 1898   Spokeshave Design

Design: Spokeshave model 1377.
Registered by: E. Preston & Sons

BT 50/324 Designs 319976-320511 1898320511 1898 July 7 – June 18

No.	322021	Class 1
Name	Edward Preston and Sons, Limited	
Address	21. Whittall Street, Birmingham	
Description	Tool Manufacturers	
Date of Registration	15th July, 1898.	

BT 51/96 Designs 319805-324854 1898 June 3 - Sept. 2

328,028   Oct. 25, 1898   Router Design

Design: Oveloe Sash with body ornamentation as seen on model 1391 spokeshaves.
Registered by: E. Preston & Sons

Class 1

Proprietors
Edwd Preston & Sons Ltd

328028

Whittall Street
Birmingham

Ornamental design for Iron Shave or router.

BT 50/335 Designs 327737-328267 1898 Oct. 20 –Oct 29

No.	328028	Class 1
Name	Edwd. Preston and Sons, Limited	
Address	Whittall Street, Birmingham.	
Description	Tool Manufacturers.	
Date of Registration	25th October, 1898	

BT 51/97 Designs 324855-329512 1898 Sept. 2 - Nov. 22

356,049   Apr. 12, 1900   Spokeshave Design

Design: Spokeshave models 1373 and 1374.
Registered by: E. Preston & Sons

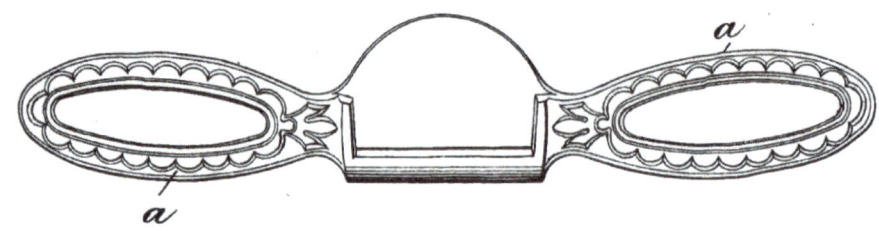

BT 50/386 Designs 355706 – 356200   1900356200 1900 Apr. 6 – Apr. 19

433	No. 356049	Class 1
Name	Edward Preston and Sons Limited	
Address	21, Whittall Street, Birmingham	
Description	Tool Manufacturers	
Date of Registration	12th April, 1900	

BT 51/103 Designs 353050-357222   1900 Feb. 9-May 14

The Evolution of the Preston Adjustable Spokeshave

The first Preston iron spokeshaves were probably made between 1875 and 1879. These spokeshaves would have had blades that were adjusted by loosening the blade fixing screw and manually advancing or retracting the blade. In 1885, Edward Preston patented an adjustment mechanism that consisted of a milled adjustment nut that had a shoulder which engaged a slot in the blade. As the milled nut was turned, the blade was either advanced or retracted. The announcement of this invention in the January 1, 1886 edition of *The British Trade Journal* showed the Preston 1392 chamfer shave with the adjuster.

IMPROVED CARPENTERS' TOOLS.

We here illustrate a new patent adjustable-stop chamfer-shave, which, among other improved carpenters' and joiners' tools, has recently been brought out by Messrs. Edward Preston & Sons, of Whittal Works, Birmingham. The first sketch shows a front and the second a back view of the new

tool. The cutting-iron, it will be seen, is adjusted by a milled nut, instead of by the hammer. A few turns of the nut will give any cut desired much more quickly and certainly than the repeated blows of the hammer applied in the old tools.

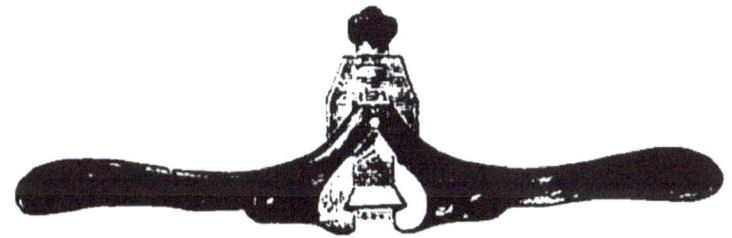

As the tool makes its own "stop" the use of the chisel is dispensed with, the chamfer and "stop" being made at the same time. The top-plate of the cutting-iron and the fences can be adjusted and fixed by the three thumbscrews shown in the first sketch. A turn-screw or screw-driver of any kind can, therefore, be dispensed with in using this tool, which also possesses other advantages, adding to the efficiency, rapidity, and nicety with which work of this class can be done.

Announcement from January 1, 1886 edition of *The British Trade Journal*

It is likely that the Preston 1390 spokeshave with solid handles was the next model to receive the adjuster. The 1390H seems to be an improvement and/or modification of the original 1390 model. The 1390H has hollow or loop handles and was first seen in the fourth edition of the Edward Preston catalogue (1891). The first version of the 1390H has smooth handles, a smooth top plate, and no lateral adjuster. All of these shaves were finished with japanning.

The original blades had a rectangular notch. Preston further improved on this mechanism by changing the shape of the notch by adding a curve to the top and bottom. This change allows the blade to be skewed to the left or to the right. This resulted in the second type of the 1390H, introduced circa 1899.

In 1898, Preston received a Registered Design Number for the embellishment of the 1390H. This resulted in the Preston 1391 spokeshave, which was available only in a nickel plated finish. The 1390H continued to be offered with plain handles and a japanned finish. At some point, perhaps around 1910, the top plate on the 1390H was chequered instead of smooth. The catalogues do not show the chequered top plate, but the chequered top plate is seen in patent documents from 1912.

In 1911, Stanley Rule and Level introduced the model 151 spokeshave. The 151 had 2 adjustment nuts that engaged the blade, thus allowing the user to skew the blade by advancing one side of the blade more than the other side. As a response, Preston developed 2 different improvements to their 1390H and 1391 spokeshaves in 1912. The first adjustment mechanism is the often seen "wing" that has been added to the adjustment nut. Pushing on one side or the other of the wing skews the blade, while the adjustment nut advances or retracts the blade. This seems to be the most commonly seen lateral adjustment mechanism on Preston spokeshaves. The fifth type of 1390H had the wing type lateral adjuster and the top plate was now of the same ornate pattern as seen on the 1391.

The other adjustment mechanism was covered by patent 20,216. This mechanism moved the adjustment nut from the body of the spokeshave to the top plate. This resulted in the model 2503 and 2504 spokeshaves. This design was also used in the Preston models 76 and 77 spokeshaves which seemed to have been introduced sometime in the 1920s. This design is still used in the convex and concave spokeshaves offered by Clifton.

In about 1914, Preston decided to give the 1390H a facelift. The 1390H now used the same casting as the 1391, but was offered in a japanned finish. The sixth type of 1390H had the ornate patterns cast into the handles. It is important to note that the 1391 was only offered with a nickel plated finish. Any spokeshave that looks like a 1391 but is either japanned or finished with a Green cellulose is a later model 1390H.

The seventh and eighth types of the 1390H were marked "PRESTON." and "ENG." on the handles. The background of the top plate is red on this type. The ninth type is painted green.

Near the end of Preston's spokeshave production (circa 1932-1933), they introduced the models 87 and 88, which were essentially copies of the Stanley model 151. After the demise of Preston, the adjustment mechanism of the 2503 and 2504 spokeshaves was used in the Clifton model 500 and 550 spokeshaves.

Tools Manufactured for the Trade

British tool dealers like Tyzack & Sons and Buck & Hickman, Ltd. typically did not identify the manufacturer of many of the tools that were listed for sale. Sometimes the only indication of the manufacturer was the name or model number that was in the artwork. In some cases the name was removed from the artwork. It appears that it was common practice to provide tools to dealers with minimal identifying marks. Several of the Preston shaves have "Preston" cast into the body of the tool, but many do not. In many cases, the only place that "Preston" or their trademark appears is on the blade. This makes it particularly difficult to identify the 1380-1384 range of tools. The body of these tools is unmarked and has a shape that is similar to tools made by other manufacturers. The problem becomes additionally challenging because tools like the Preston's Patent Punch Saw Set (Preston 1460) appears in the 1909 William Marples catalogue as if it were a Marples product. This would seem to indicate that tools were made by one manufacturer and then distributed through other manufacturers.

Marples, Mathieson, Moseley & Son, C & P Parks, and Kimberley were manufacturers that made and/or sold shaves and routers that can easily be mistaken for Preston tools. Versions of the 1385 chamfer shave, the 1386 improved circular rabbeting and fillister router, 1387 series improved circular sash routers, 1388 quirk router, and 1389 series circular bead routers that appear to have not been manufactured by Preston have been observed. In many cases, the only clue to the manufacturer is the name that is stamped in the blade.

In the 1899 Alex Mathieson catalogue, lists the following sash shaves:

- 824, sash shave, iron, gothic in ½, $^5/_8$, and ¾ inch
- 825, sash shave, iron, ovalo in ½, $^9/_{16}$, $^5/_8$, and ¾ inch
- 826, sash shave, iron, lambtongue in ½, $^9/_{16}$, $^5/_8$, and ¾ inch

Notice that Mathieson describes the profile of the #825 router as ovalo whereas Preston describes the profile as oveloe. Although the Mathieson sash shaves are similar to Preston sash shaves, there are distinct differences in the casting of the Mathieson sash shaves.

Sash routers with blades marked D Kimberley have been observed. No catalogues for D Kimberley have been found. David Kimberley and D Kimberley & Sons are listed in W.L. Goodman's *British Plane Makers from 1700* at various addresses in Birmingham from 1854 to 1906. An article in *Engineering*, volume 81, dated March 30, 1906 states, "Messrs. Wynn, Timmins, and Co., Limited, Commercial street, Birmingham, have bought the goodwill, name, and trademarks &c. of the firm of the late D. Kimberley and Sons, Limited, tool manufacturers, Emily Street and Angelina Street, Highgate, Birmingham." No sash routers have been observed marked Wynn, Timmins, and Co. It is not known if the manufacture of the Kimberley sash routers was continued under the Kimberley name or if production ceased. The castings of the Kimberley sash routers seem to be identical to the Preston castings but the profile that is machined into the router is distinctly different from the same profile of a Preston sash router. It is unknown if Kimberley purchased raw castings from Preston. If they did, Kimberley must have done the finishing themselves.

Marples sold versions of the 1387 series sash routers, the 1386 circular rabbeting router, and 1388 quirk routers. The fence screws on all observed tools with a Marples blade were $9/32$ inch BSW, while the fence screws on all observed tools with Preston markings are ¼ inch BSW. As such, it appears that although the castings are very similar, to the extent that they may have all come from the same source, the finishing does appear to differ between the firms that sold the tool.

Beading shaves with blades marked MOSELEY & SON have been observed. William Marples purchased Moseley & Son in 1892.

76 Iron Spokeshave

Description

The 76 and 77 are essentially the same spokeshave. The difference is that the 76 is the round faced version and the 77 is the flat faced version. The adjustment mechanism on the model 76 and model 77 spokeshaves are similar to the adjustment mechanism on the model 2502 and 2503 spokeshaves. These spokeshaves were introduced in catalogue 26R, which was probably published in the early 1920s. The model 76 spokeshave was listed in *Preston Catalogue No. 43* (1932) and *John Rabone & Sons Catalogue No. 27* (1933). The Rabone catalogue indicated that Rabone had purchased Preston.

Dimensions

Length: 9 $^{15}/_{16}$ inches
Blade width: 2$^{1}/_{8}$ inches
Weight: 25 $^{1}/_{4}$ oz.

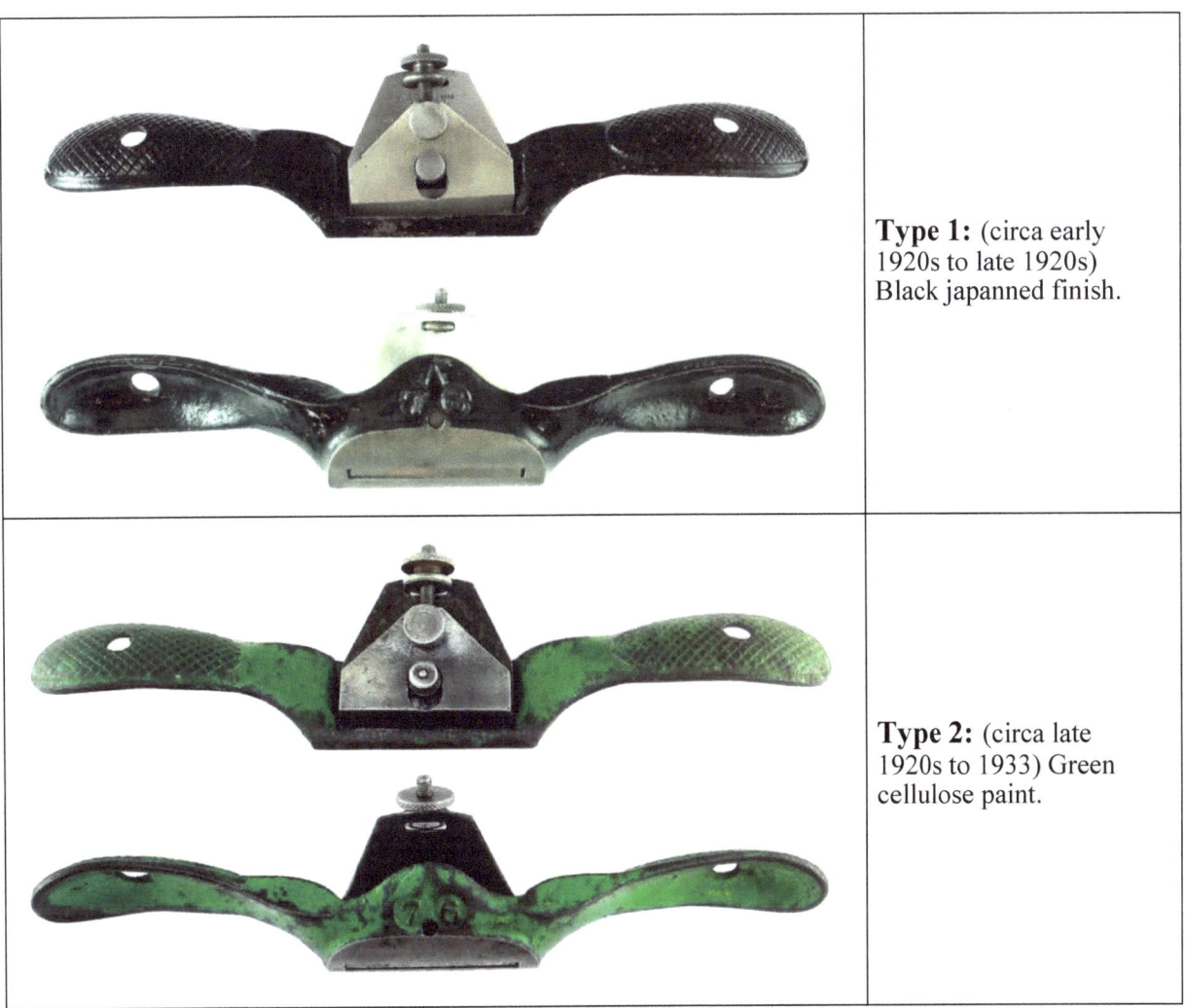

	Type 1: (circa early 1920s to late 1920s) Black japanned finish.
	Type 2: (circa late 1920s to 1933) Green cellulose paint.

77 Iron Spokeshave

Description

The 76 and 77 are essentially the same spokeshave. The difference is that the 76 is the round faced version and the 77 is the flat faced version. These spokeshaves were introduced in catalogue 26R, which was probably published in the early 1920s. The model 76 spokeshave was listed in *Preston Catalogue No. 43* (1932) and *John Rabone & Sons Catalogue No. 27* (1933). The Rabone catalogue indicated that Rabone had purchased Preston.

Dimensions
Length: 9 $^{15}/_{16}$ inches
Blade width: 2$^1/_8$ inches
Weight: 25 $^1/_4$ oz.

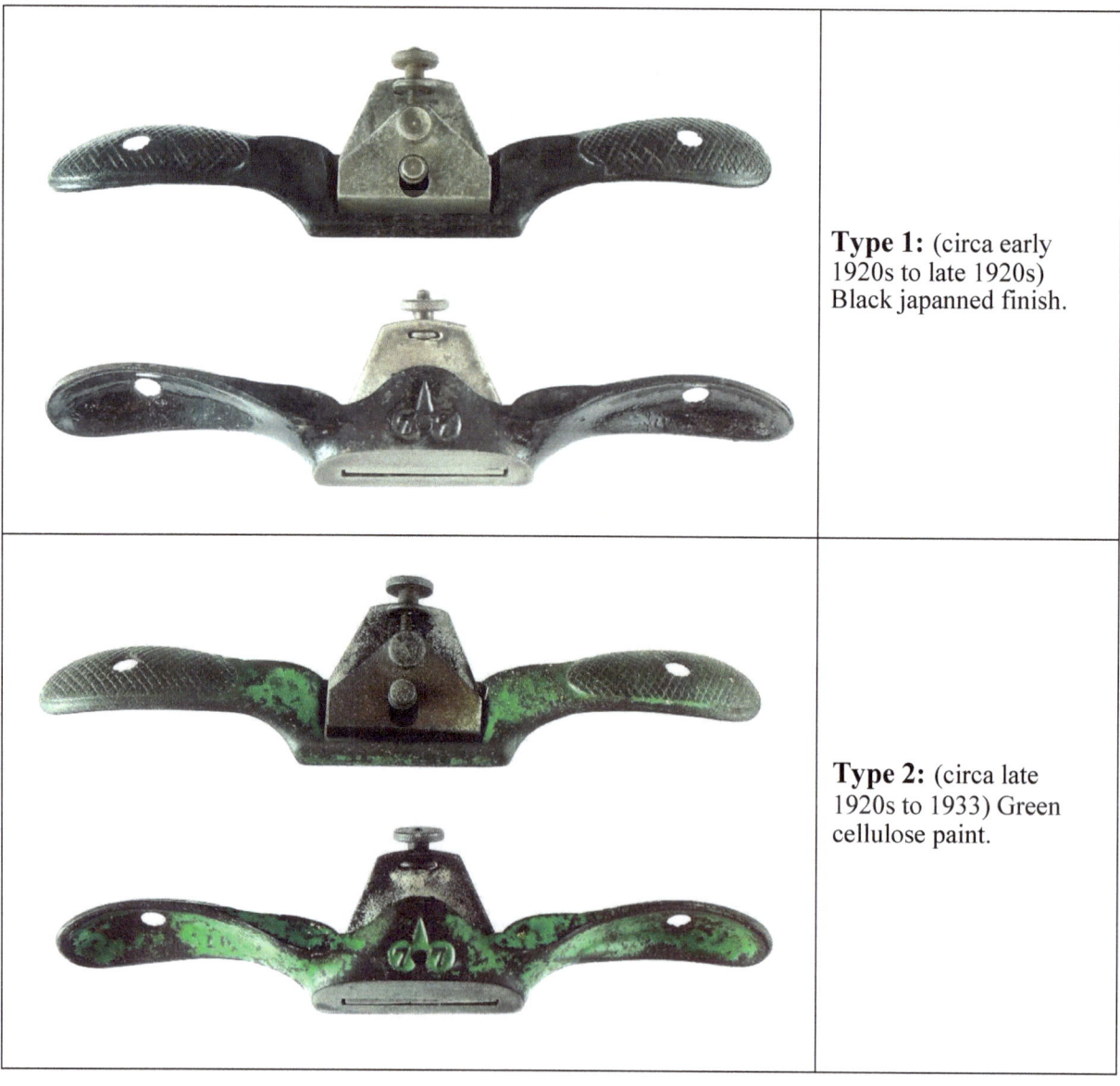

	Type 1: (circa early 1920s to late 1920s) Black japanned finish.
	Type 2: (circa late 1920s to 1933) Green cellulose paint.

78 Iron Spokeshave

Description

The 78 and 79 are essentially the same spokeshave. The difference is that the 78 is the round faced version and the 79 is the flat faced version. These shaves are the updated versions of the 1379 and were introduced in catalogue 26R, which was probably published in the early 1920s. The model 78 spokeshave was listed in *Preston Catalogue No. 43* (1932) and *John Rabone & Sons Catalogue No. 27* (1933). The Rabone catalogue indicated that Rabone had purchased Preston.

Dimensions

Length: 8 ⅝ inches to 8¾ inches
Blade width: 1 ¹³/₁₆ inches
Weight: 6 oz.

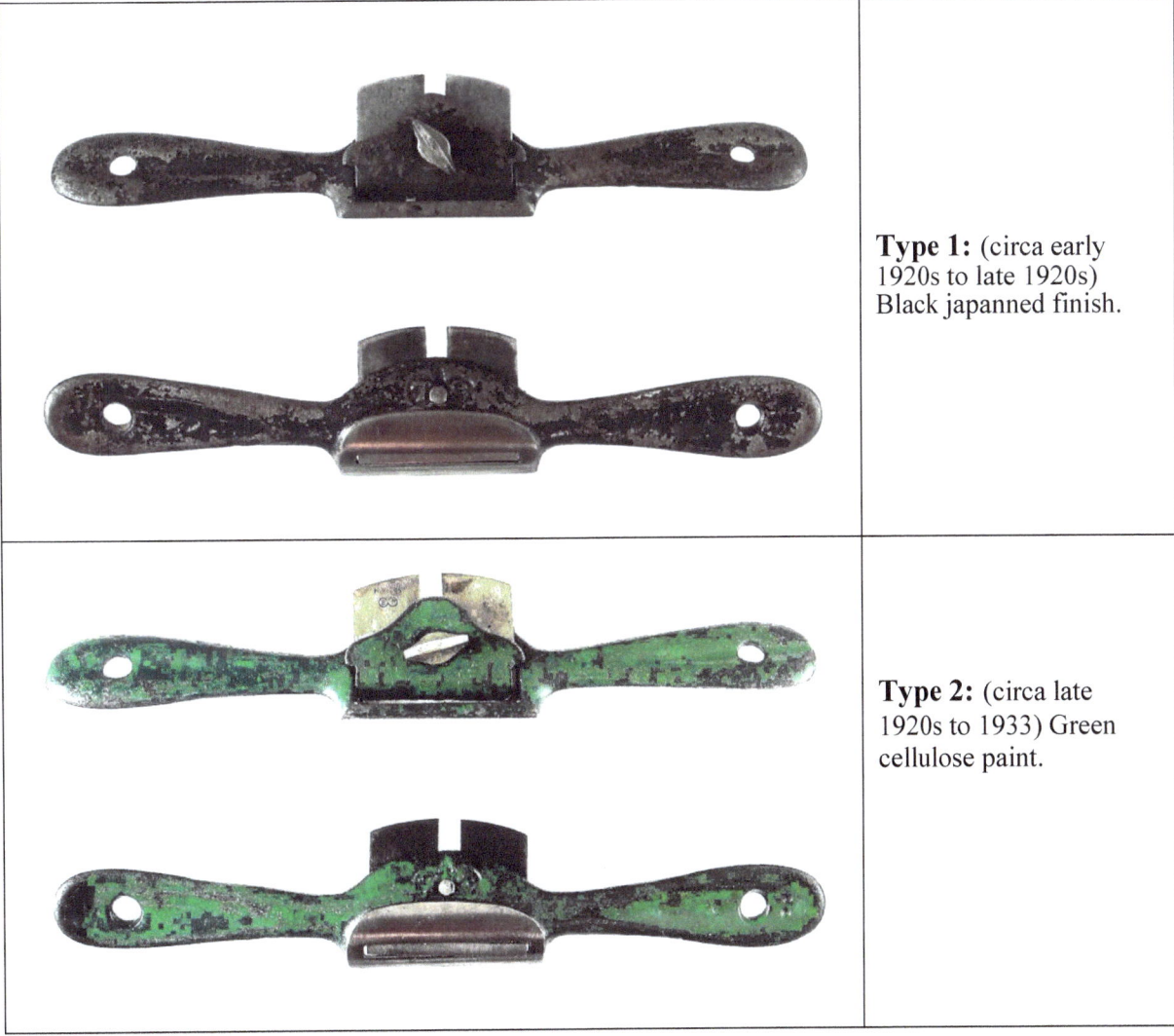

	Type 1: (circa early 1920s to late 1920s) Black japanned finish.
	Type 2: (circa late 1920s to 1933) Green cellulose paint.

79 Iron Spokeshave

Description

The 78 and 79 are essentially the same spokeshave. The difference is that the 78 is the round faced version and the 79 is the flat faced version. These shaves are the updated versions of the 1379 and were introduced in catalogue 26R, which was probably published in the early 1920s. The model 78 spokeshave was listed in *Preston Catalogue No. 43* (1932) and *John Rabone & Sons Catalogue No. 27* (1933). The Rabone catalogue indicated that Rabone had purchased Preston.

Dimensions

Length: 8 ⅝ inches to 8¾ inches
Blade width: 1 ¹³⁄₁₆ inches
Weight: 6 ⅓ oz.

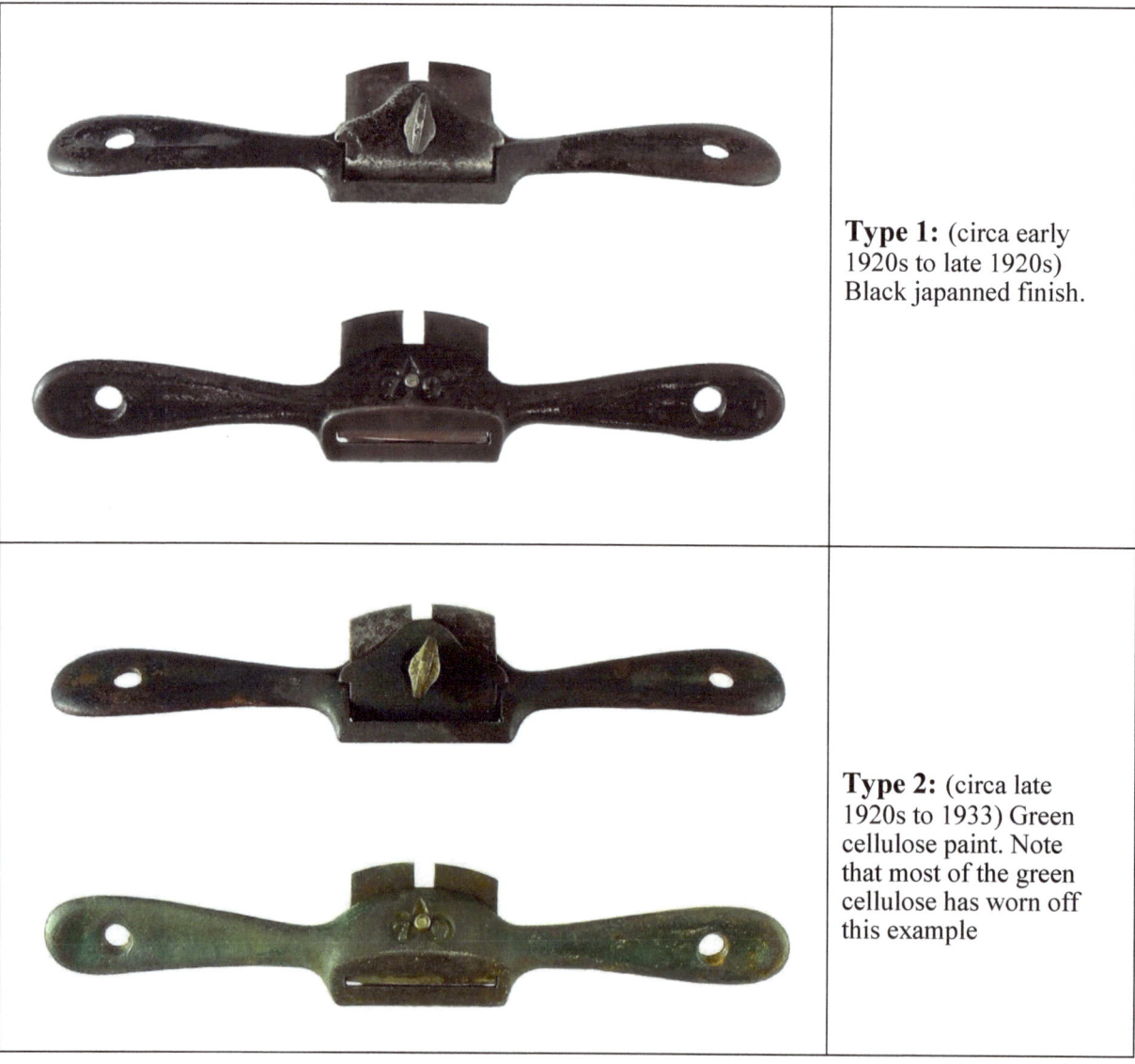

	Type 1: (circa early 1920s to late 1920s) Black japanned finish.
	Type 2: (circa late 1920s to 1933) Green cellulose paint. Note that most of the green cellulose has worn off this example

24

80 Iron Spokeshave

Description

The 80 and 81 are essentially the same spokeshave. The difference is that the 80 is the round faced version and the 81 is the flat faced version. These shaves are the updated versions of the 1381 ½ and were introduced in catalogue 26R, which was probably published in the early 1920s. The model 80 and model 81 spokeshaves are listed in the 1925 Richard Melhuish catalogue. The model 80 spokeshave was listed in *Preston Catalogue No. 43* (1932) and *John Rabone & Sons Catalogue No. 27* (1933). The Rabone catalogue indicated that Rabone had purchased Preston.

Dimensions

Length: 9 $^{13}/_{16}$ inches
Blade width: 2$^{1}/_{8}$ inches
Weight: 10 oz.

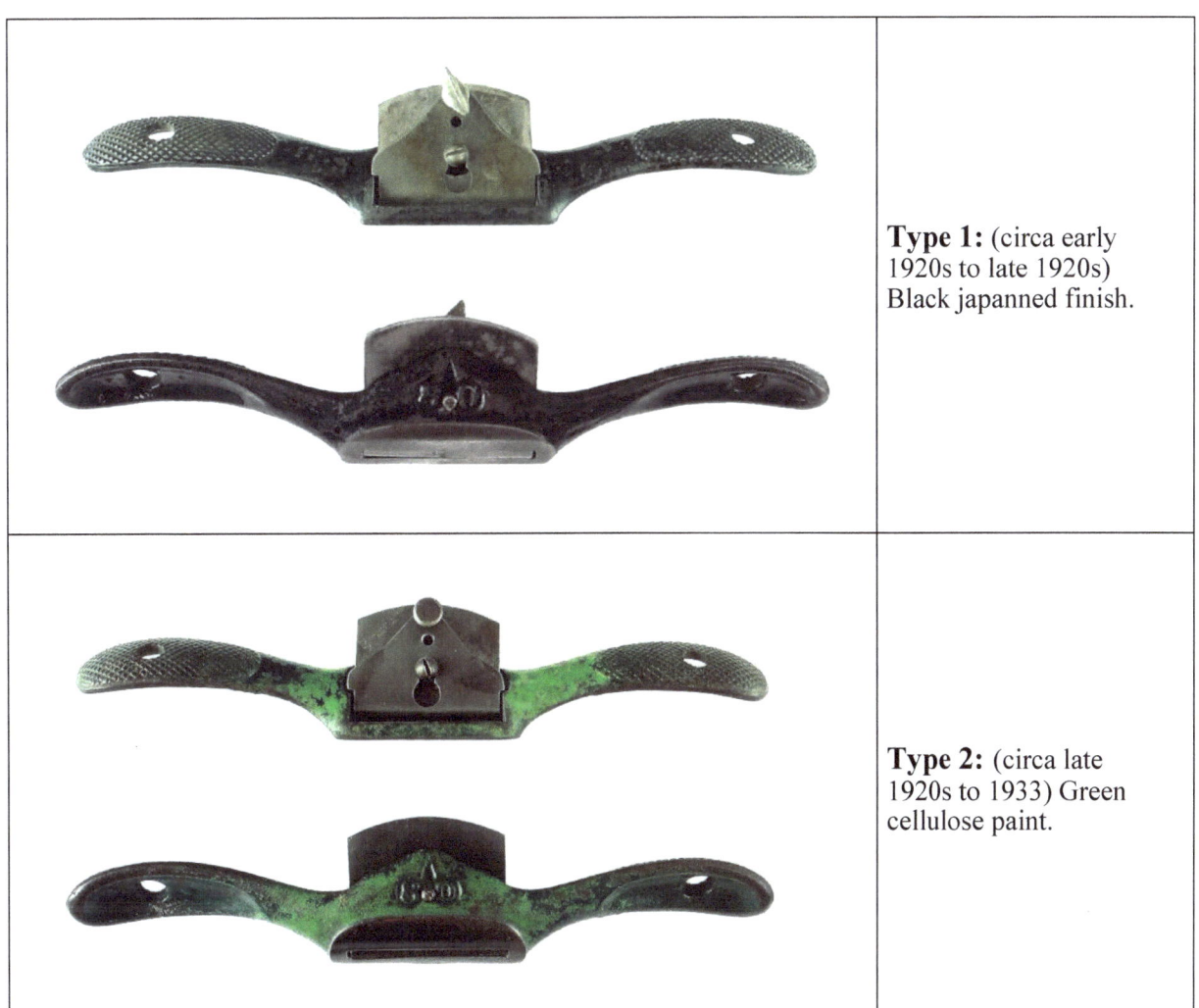

	Type 1: (circa early 1920s to late 1920s) Black japanned finish.
	Type 2: (circa late 1920s to 1933) Green cellulose paint.

81 Iron Spokeshave

Description

The 80 and 81 are essentially the same spokeshave. The difference is that the 80 is the round faced version and the 81 is the flat faced version. These shaves are the updated versions of the 1381 ½ and were introduced in catalogue 26R, which was probably published in the early 1920s. The model 80 and model 81 spokeshaves are listed in the 1925 Richard Melhuish catalogue. The model 80 spokeshave was listed in *Preston Catalogue No. 43* (1932) and *John Rabone & Sons Catalogue No. 27* (1933). The Rabone catalogue indicated that Rabone had purchased Preston.

Dimensions

Length: 9 $^{15}/_{16}$ inches
Blade width: 2$^{1}/_{8}$ inches
Weight: 10 $^{3}/_{4}$ oz.

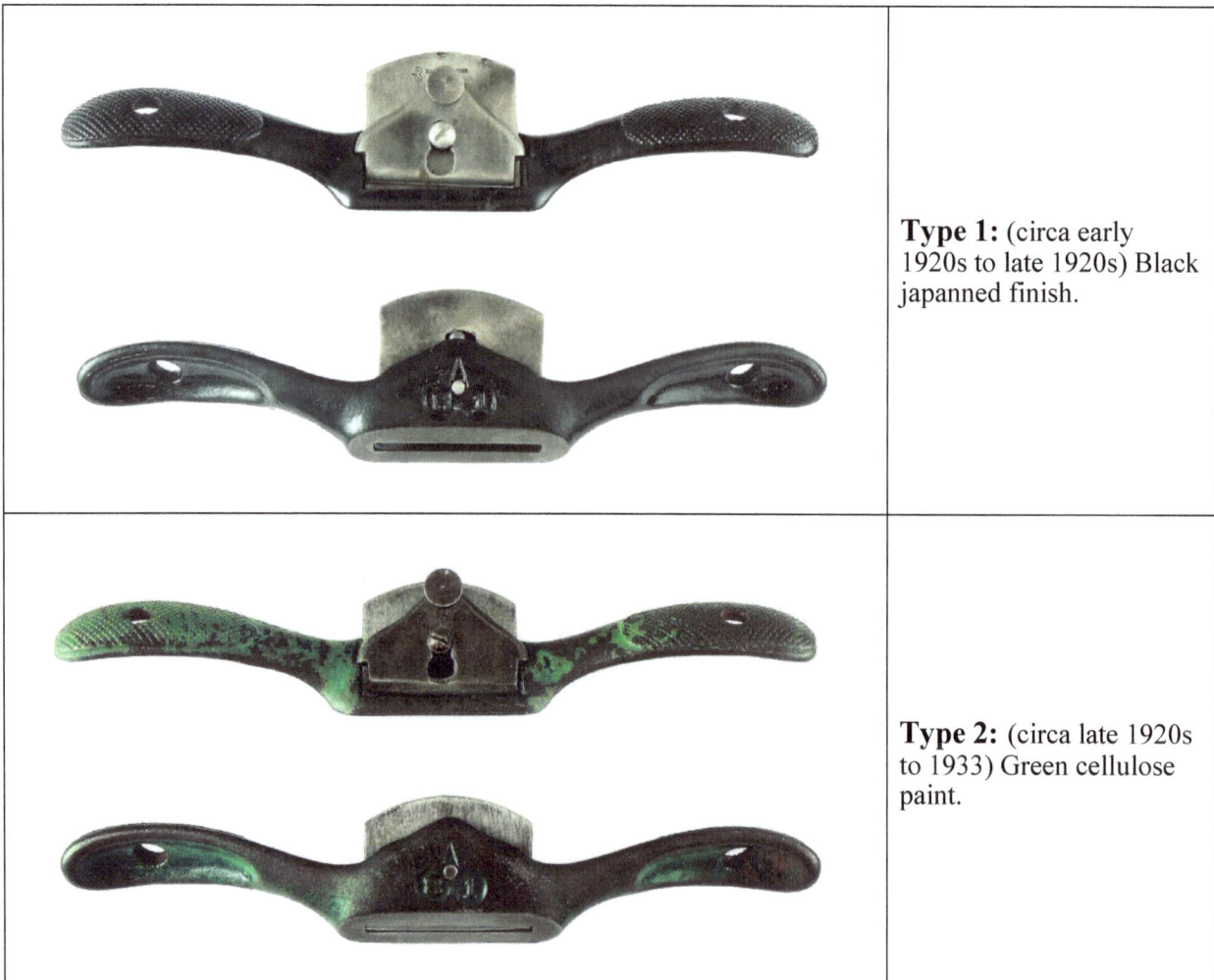

	Type 1: (circa early 1920s to late 1920s) Black japanned finish.
	Type 2: (circa late 1920s to 1933) Green cellulose paint.

82 Adjustable Mouth Iron Spokeshave

Description

The model 82 is an updated version of the 1382 ½ and was introduced in catalogue 26R, which was probably published in the early 1920s. The model 82 spokeshave was listed in *Preston Catalogue No. 43* (1932) and *John Rabone & Sons Catalogue No. 27* (1933). The Rabone catalogue indicated that Rabone had purchased Preston.

Dimensions

Length: 10 ¼ inches
Blade width: $2^{1}/_{8}$ inches
Weight: $12\,^{2}/_{3}$ oz.

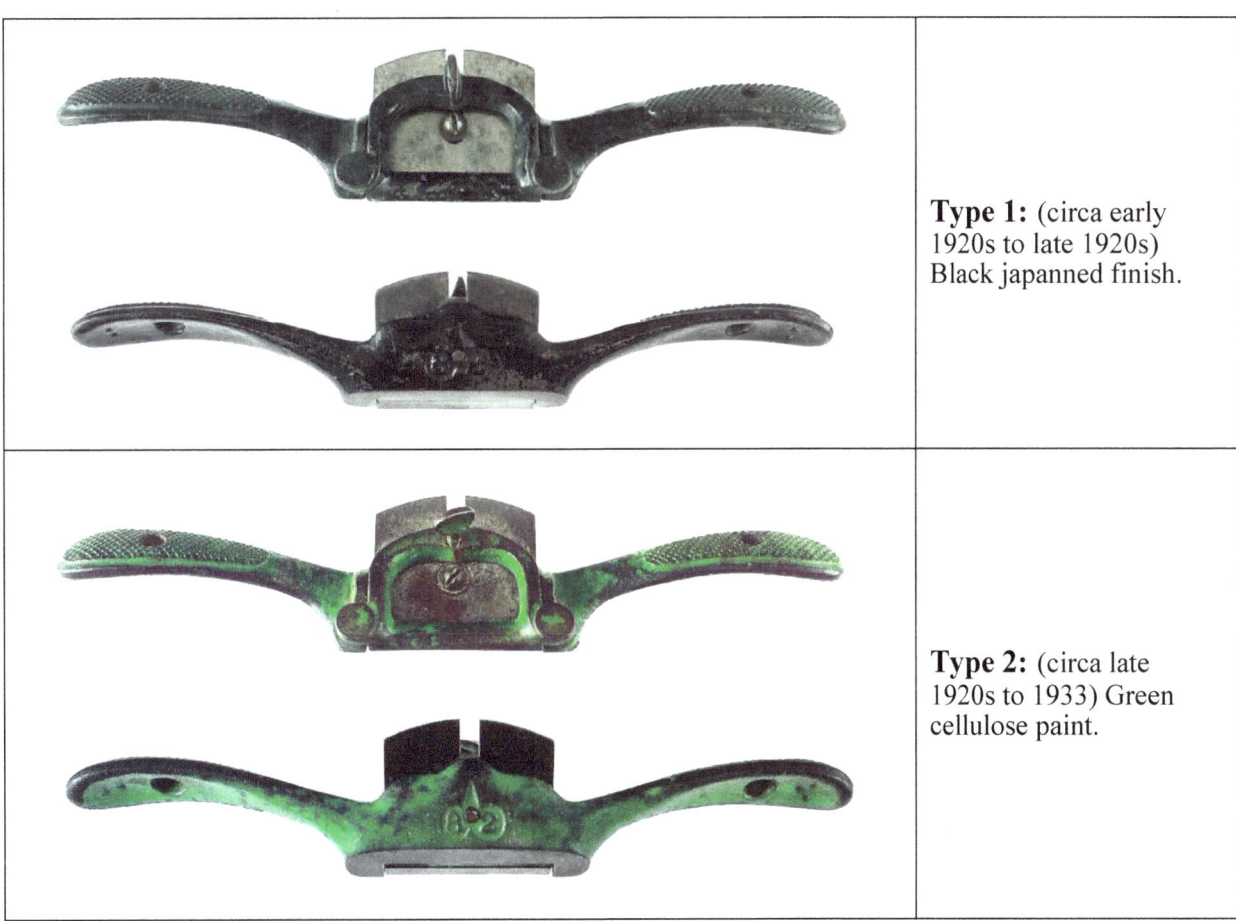

	Type 1: (circa early 1920s to late 1920s) Black japanned finish.
	Type 2: (circa late 1920s to 1933) Green cellulose paint.

83 Iron Spokeshave

Description

This spokeshave is a concave spokeshave similar to the model 1383. The difference between the 1383 and the 83 is that the 83 has chequered handles similar to the handles on the models 87, 88, and 89 spokeshaves. The model 83 spokeshave was listed in *Preston Catalogue No. 43* (1932) and *John Rabone & Sons Catalogue No. 27* (1933).

Dimensions

Length: 10 inches
Blade width: 2 $\frac{1}{8}$ inches
Weight: not available

No. 83

Raised Chequered Handle.
10 inches long. 2⅛ inch **Cutting Iron**.

No. 83 Hollow Face   ...   25/- per dozen.

Rabone Catalogue No. 27 (1933)

87 Iron Spokeshave

Description

The model 87 spokeshave is the round faced version of the model 88 spokeshave. This spokeshave was not listed in *Preston Catalogue No. 43* (1932). It was listed in *John Rabone & Sons Catalogue No. 27* (1933). This would indicate that the model 87 spokeshave was introduced in the very last days before Rabone had purchased Preston. It was only produced with a green cellulose finish.

Dimensions

Length: 10$^{1}/_{8}$ inches
Blade width: 2$^{1}/_{8}$ inches
Weight: 12 $^{2}/_{3}$ oz.

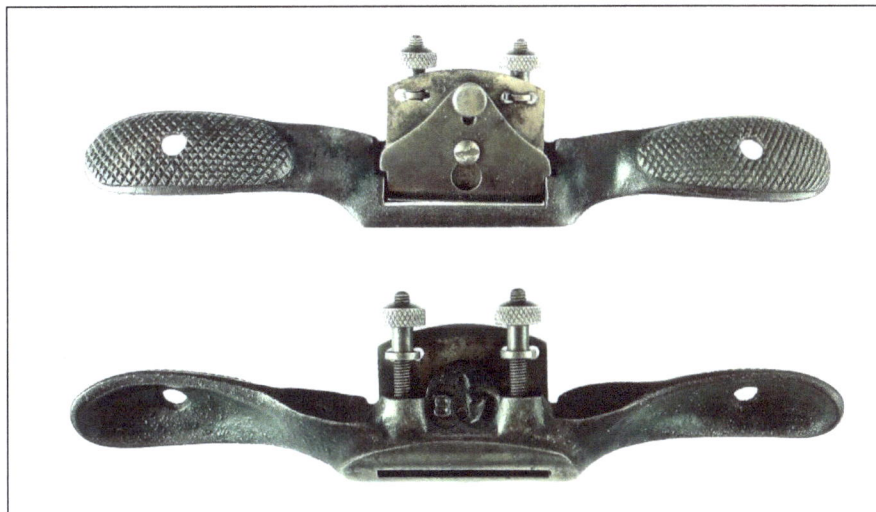

The model 87 spokeshave has only been observed with a green cellulose finish. (circa 1933)

88 Iron Spokeshave

Description

The model 88 spokeshave is the flat faced version of the model 87 spokeshave. It was introduced prior to the model 87. The model 88 appears to be more common than the 87. The model 88 spokeshave was listed in *Preston Catalogue No. 43* (1932) and *John Rabone & Sons Catalogue No. 27* (1933). The Rabone catalogue indicated that Rabone had purchased Preston. The model 88 has only been observed with a green cellulose finish.

Dimensions

Length: $10^{1}/_{8}$ inches
Blade width: $2^{1}/_{8}$ inches
Weight: $12^{\,2}/_{3}$ oz.

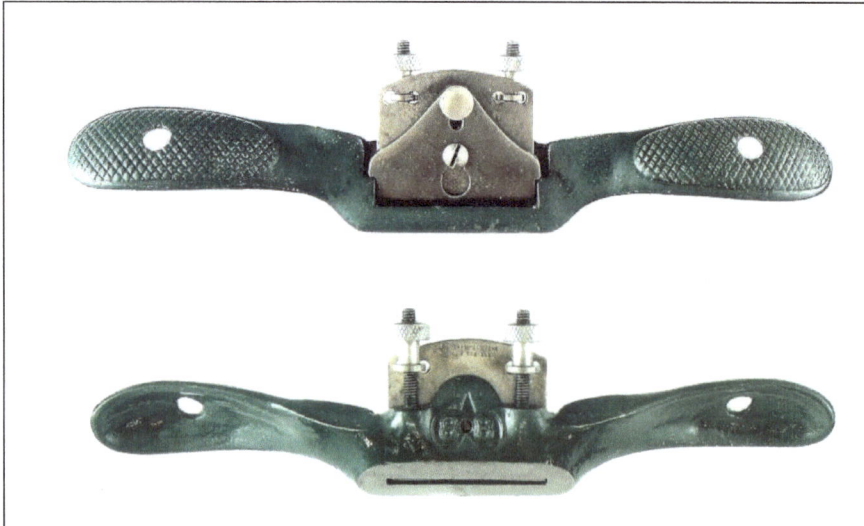

The model 88 spokeshave has only been observed with a green cellulose finish. (circa 1932 to 1933)

89 Iron Chamfer Spokeshave

Description

The Preston No. 89 Chamfer spokeshave appears to be the predecessor to the Record A65. The Record A65 was made from 1954 to 1965. The Preston 89 and Record A65 appear to be very similar to the Stanley 65. This spokeshave was not listed in *Preston Catalogue No. 43*, dated October 1932. It was listed in the 1933 John Rabone & Sons catalogue. This would indicate that the model 89 spokeshave was introduced in the very last days before Rabone had purchased Preston. The 1933 Rabone catalogue indicated that Rabone had purchased Preston. The model 89 spokeshave was only made with a green cellulose finish.

Dimensions

Length: 10 $^1/_8$ inches
Blade width: 1 ½ inches
Weight: 12 $^1/_3$ oz.

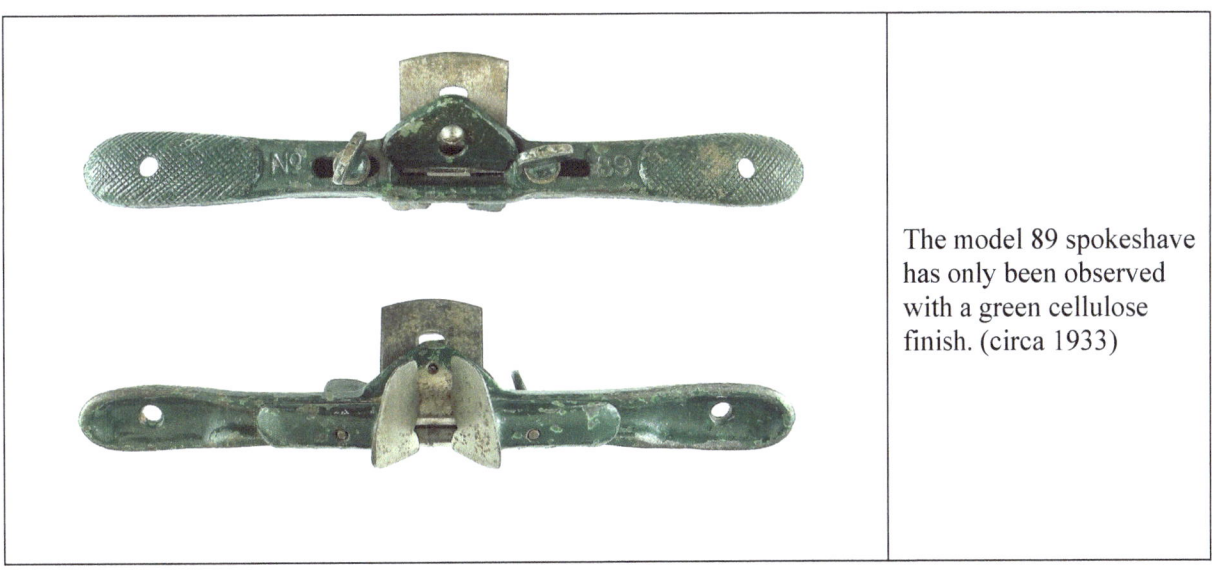

The model 89 spokeshave has only been observed with a green cellulose finish. (circa 1933)

180 Cabinet Scraper

Description

The Preston No. 180 cabinet scraper is similar in design to the Stanley No. 80 cabinet scraper. This tool was not included in *Preston Catalogue No. 43*, dated October 1932. It is likely that this tool was introduced in late 1932 or early 1933.

Dimensions

Length: 11 ½ inches
Blade width: 2 ½ inches
Weight: 24 $^1/_8$ oz.

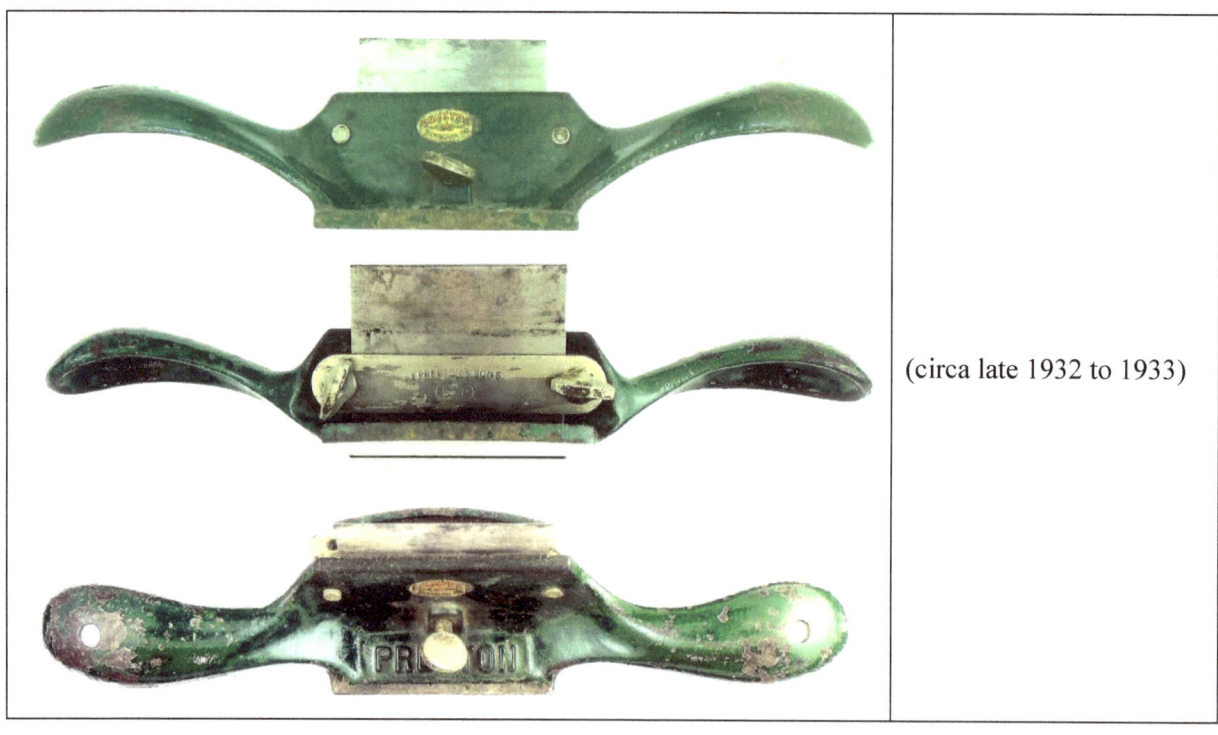

(circa late 1932 to 1933)

1373 Registered Iron Spokeshave

Description

The registered number on the 1373 spokeshave was issued April 12, 1900. As no examples of this spokeshave have been observed without the registered number and the 1373 is listed in the 1901 Preston catalogue, production of this spokeshave must have begun between 1900 and 1901. The 1373 remained in production until Preston ceased trading in 1932. The catalogue describes the 1373 as "Hollow raised handles, malleable Iron, nickel plated, 6 inch, round face, 1 inch cutting iron".

Dimensions

Length: 5 $^7/_8$ inches
Blade width: $^{31}/_{32}$ inches
Weight: 3 oz.

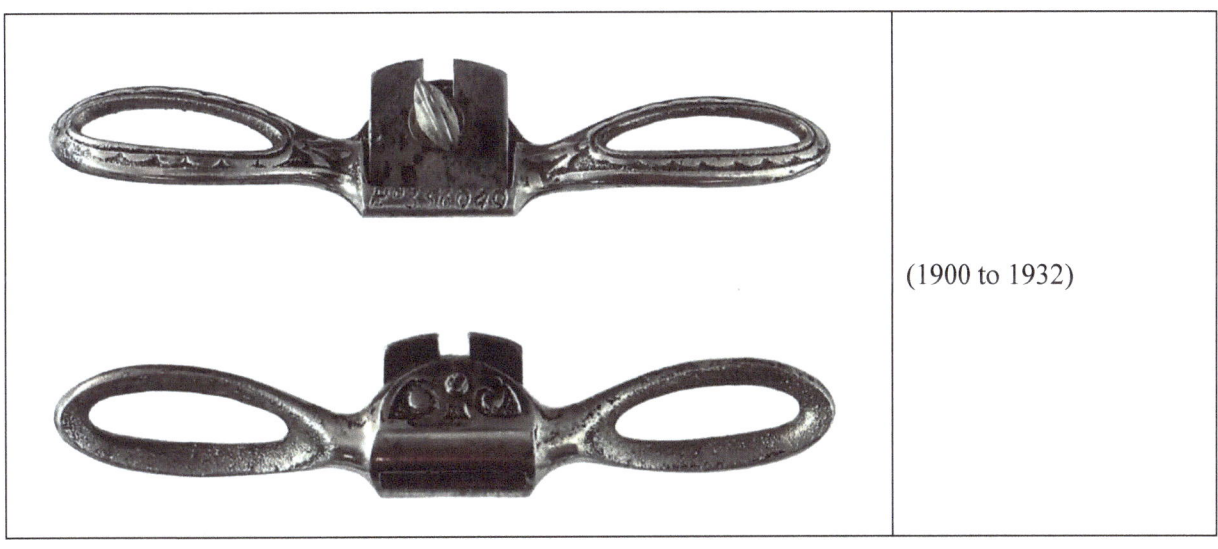

(1900 to 1932)

1374 Registered Iron Spokeshave

Description

The registered number on the 1374 spokeshave was issued April 12, 1900. As no examples of this spokeshave have been observed without the registered number and the 1374 is listed in the 1901 Preston catalogue, production of this spokeshave must have begun between 1900 and 1901. The 1374 remained in production until Preston ceased trading in 1932.

Dimensions

Length: 6 $^{15}/_{16}$ inches
Blade width: 1 $^{7}/_{16}$ inches
Weight: 4 oz.

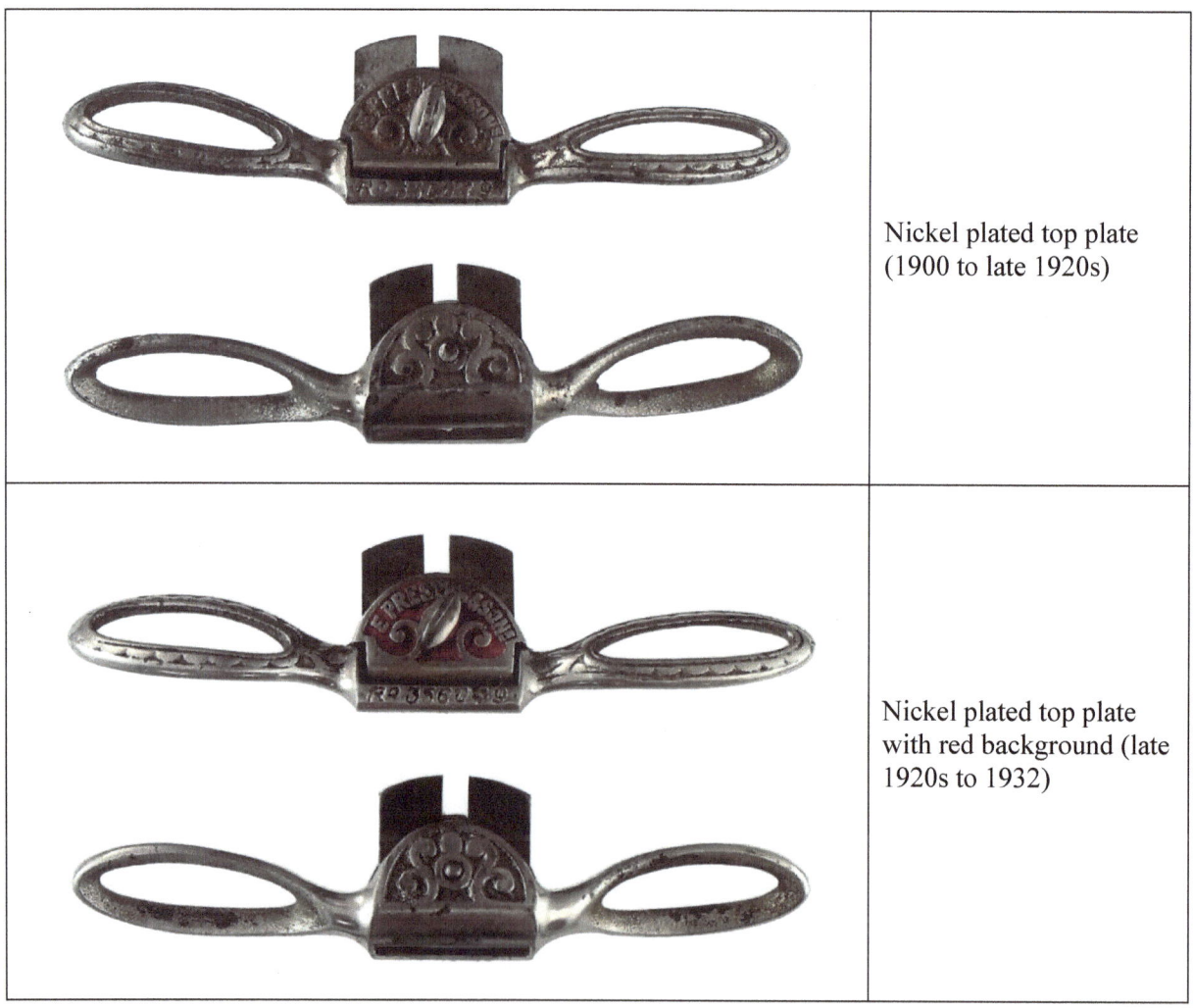

	Nickel plated top plate (1900 to late 1920s)
	Nickel plated top plate with red background (late 1920s to 1932)

1374P Registered Iron Spokeshave

Description

The 1374P is essentially a 1374 with the addition of the Preston depth adjuster. This shave was never offered with the lateral adjuster. The 1374P was introduced between 1900 and 1901. It remained in production until Preston ceased trading in 1932. Preston catalogues only show that the 1374P was available with a round face; however, the author has multiple examples of the 1374P with a flat face. There are examples of this spokeshave that have a smooth back instead of an ornate one.

Dimensions

Length: 8 $^7/_{16}$ inches
Blade width: 1 $^7/_{16}$ inches
Weight: 5 $^2/_3$ oz.

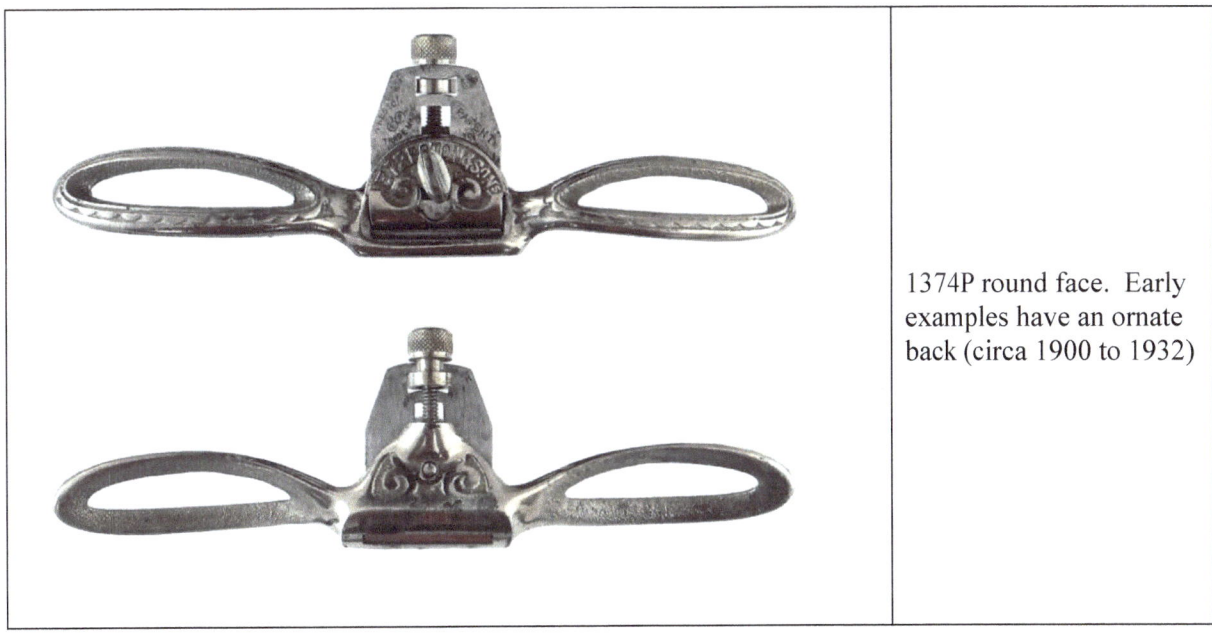

1374P round face. Early examples have an ornate back (circa 1900 to 1932)

	1374P flat face with ornate back (circa 1900 to 1932)
	1374P round face. Later examples have a smooth back. It is unknown when this change was introduced (circa 1900 to 1932)

1377 Patent Iron Spokeshave

Description

The registered number on the 1377 spokeshave was issued July 15, 1898. As no examples of this spokeshave have been observed without the registered number and the 1377 is listed in the 1901 Preston catalogue, production of this spokeshave must have begun between 1898 and 1901. This spokeshave remained in production until Preston ceased trading in 1932. The 1377T was the same spokeshave but with a "Thumbscrew to top plate". This was seen in the 1909 catalogue, but this option was not in the 1914 Preston catalogue.

A flat faced variation was acquired in the January 2011 Brown Tool Auction but at this time it is unclear if this spokeshave was modified after it left the factory. No other flat faced 1377's have been seen and there are no known catalogue references. The flat face appears to be nickel plated indicating that it was plated after any modifications to the face

Dimensions

Length: 7 $^{1}/_{16}$ inches
Blade width: 1 $^{7}/_{16}$ inches
Weight: 4 $^{3}/_{4}$ oz.

1377 round face. Early examples have an ornate back (circa 1898 to late 1920s)

	1377 flat face (circa 1898 to 1932)
	1377 round face and smooth back. It is unknown when this change was introduced, but examples with a smooth back seem to be less common. (circa 1898 to late 1920s)
	1377T with plated top plate. It is unknown when this change was introduced, but examples with a smooth back seem to be less common. (circa 1898 to late 1920s)

	1377 round face with red background on top plate, smooth back (circa late 1920s to 1932)
	1377T with red top plate (circa late 1920s to 1932)

Unidentified Early Preston Iron Spokeshave

Description

This spokeshave appears to be fairly common but does not appear in the 1891, 1895, 1901, 1909, 1914, and 1932 Preston catalogues. This spokeshave is only seen with a japanned finish and the blade on this spokeshave is either marked "PRESTON" over "BIRM$^{\underline{M}}$ ENG" or "PRESTON" over "TRADEMARK". These markings are consistent with those used prior to 1891. These characteristics indicate that the production of this spokeshave was between the 1870s and 1890. If this spokeshave was included in early Preston catalogues, it was withdrawn prior to 1891.

Dimensions

Length: 9 $^1/_8$ inches
Blade width: 1 $^3/_4$ inches
Weight: 8 $^1/_8$ oz.

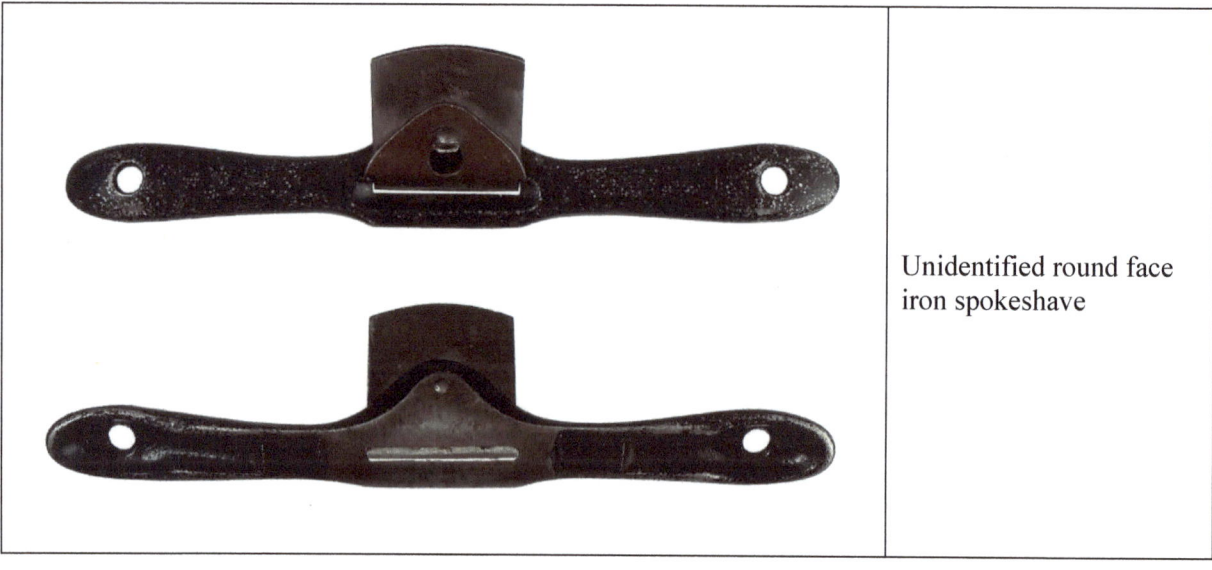

Unidentified round face iron spokeshave

1379 Iron Spokeshave

Description

The model 1379 spokeshave appears in a Preston advertisement in the October 1, 1880 edition of *The British Trade Journal*. As such, Preston would have started production of this model spokeshave no later than 1880. Production continued until the 1379 was replaced with the models 78 and 79 spokeshaves, probably in the 1920s. The 78 and 79 are essentially the same as the 1379 with the exception that the model number is cast into the body of the spokeshave

Dimensions

Length: 8 $^7/_8$ inches
Blade width: 1 $^7/_{16}$ inches
Weight: 5 $^3/_4$ oz.

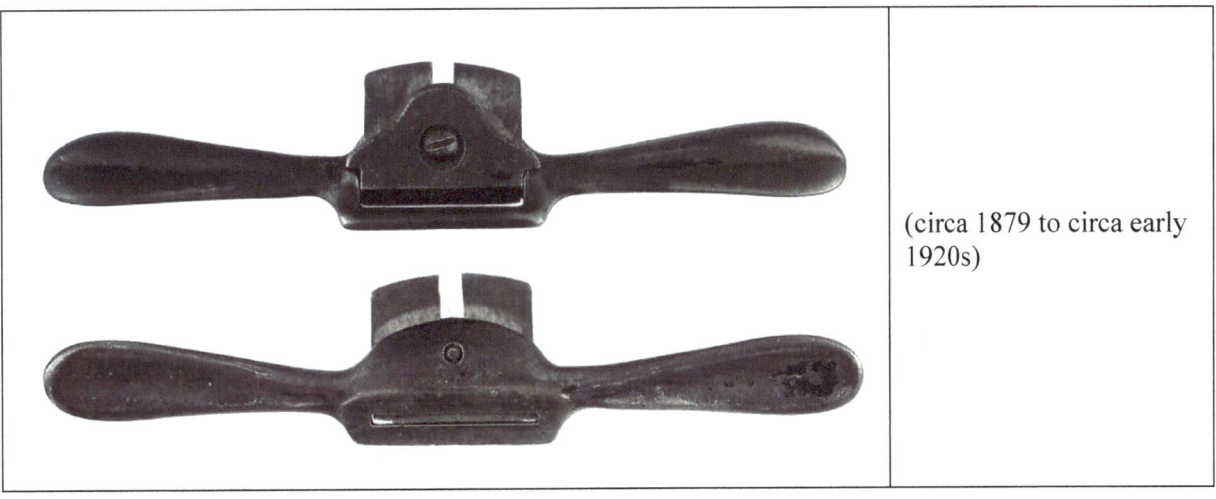

(circa 1879 to circa early 1920s)

1380 Iron Spokeshave

Description

The No. 1380 spokeshave was likely introduced around 1879. It appears to be a copy of Bailey's No. 8 spokeshave. This spokeshave was discontinued, most likely in the 1920s.

Dimensions

Length: 10 ½ inches
Blade width: 2 $^1/_{16}$ inches
Weight: 9 $^3/_4$ oz.

1380 flat face (circa 1879 to circa early 1920s)

1380 ½ Iron Spokeshave

Description

The No. 1380 ½ spokeshave was likely introduced around 1879. This spokeshave was eventually replaced by the Nos. 80 and 81 spokeshaves, probably in the 1920s.

Dimensions

Length: 10 ⅛ inches
Blade width: 2 ¹⁄₁₆ inches
Weight: 10 ½ oz.

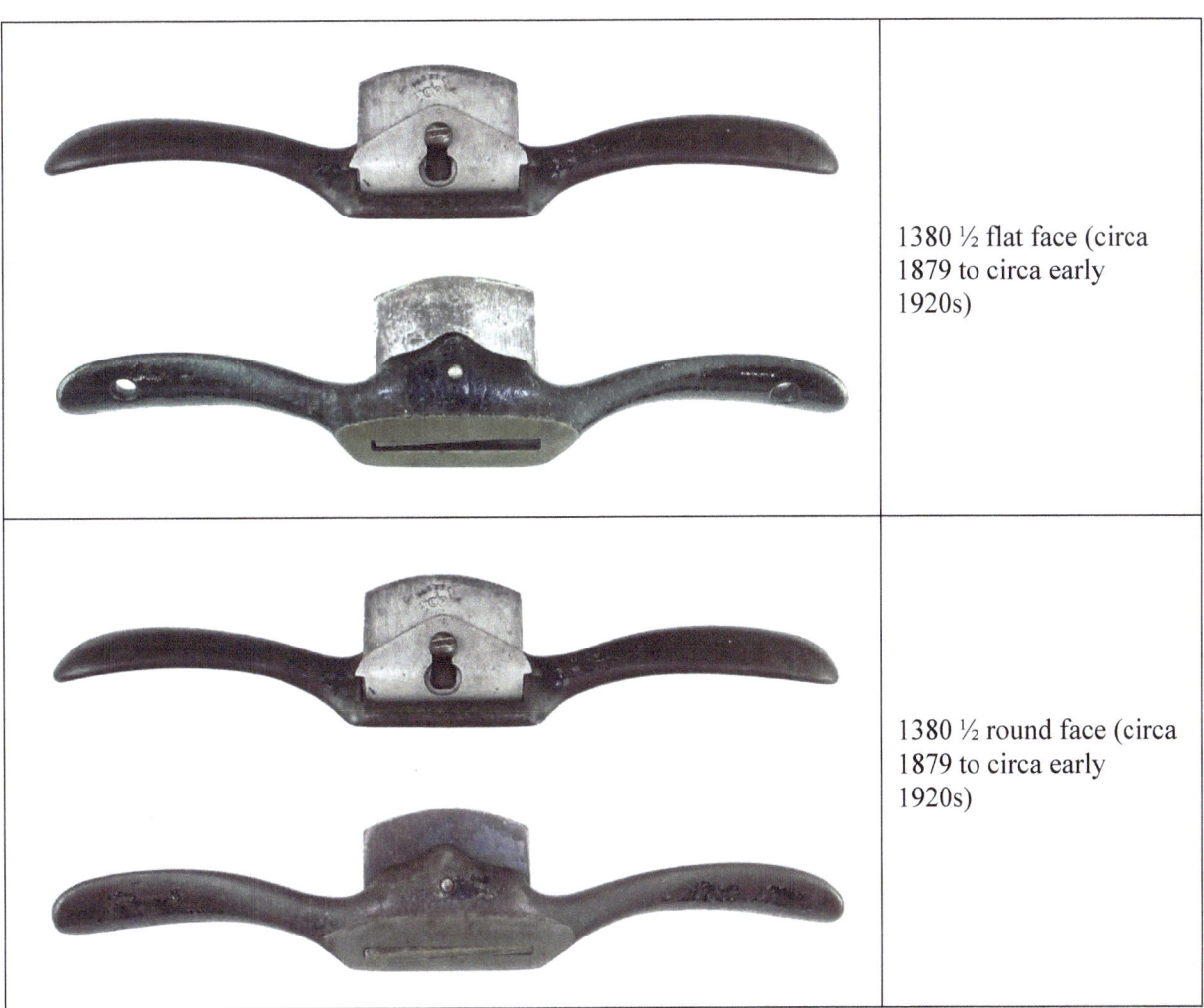

	1380 ½ flat face (circa 1879 to circa early 1920s)
	1380 ½ round face (circa 1879 to circa early 1920s)

1381 Iron Spokeshave

Description

The No. 1381 spokeshave was likely introduced around 1879. It appears to be a copy of Bailey's No. 2 spokeshave. This spokeshave was discontinued, most likely in the 1920s.

Dimensions

Length: 9 $^7/_8$ inches
Blade width: 2 $^1/_{16}$ inches
Weight: 9 $^2/_3$ oz.

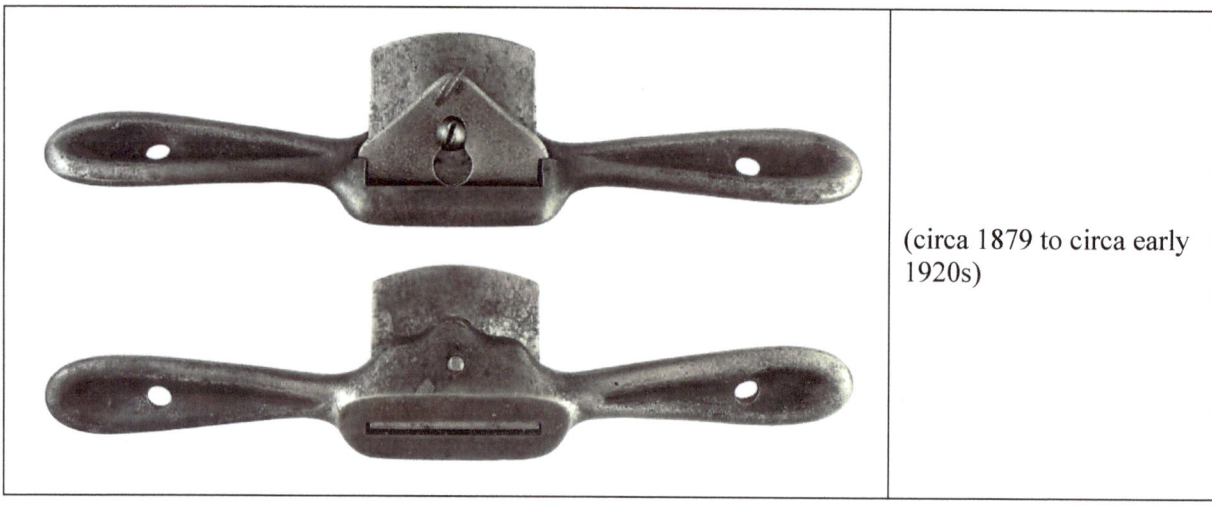

(circa 1879 to circa early 1920s)

1381 ½ Iron Spokeshave

Description

The No. 1381 ½ spokeshave was likely introduced around 1879. It appears to be a copy of Bailey's No. 1 spokeshave. This spokeshave was discontinued, most likely with the introduction of the Nos. 80 and 81 spokeshaves in the 1920s.

Dimensions

Length: 10 ¼ inches
Blade width: 2 $^{1}/_{16}$ inches
Weight: 10 $^{7}/_{8}$ oz.

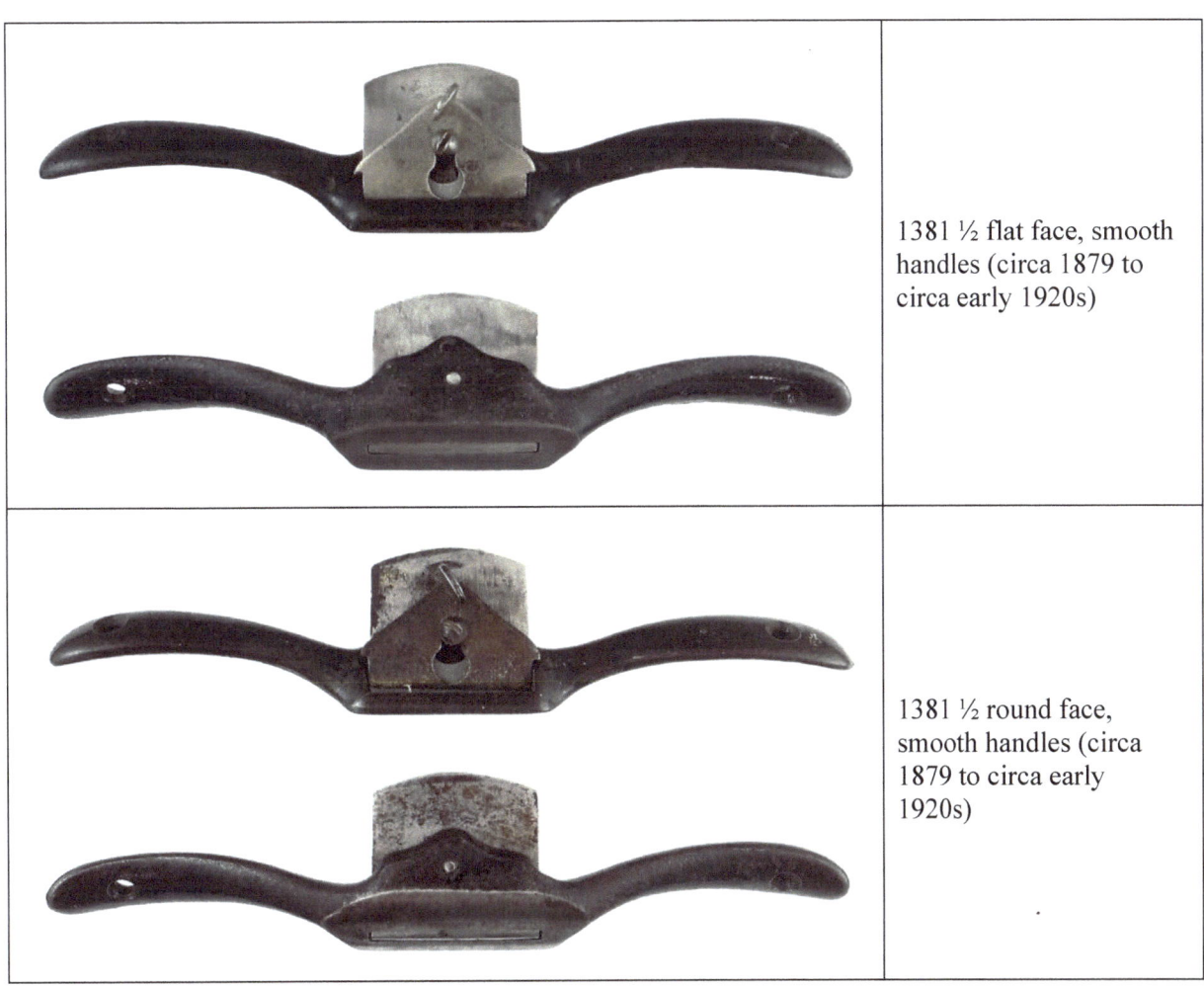

	1381 ½ flat face, smooth handles (circa 1879 to circa early 1920s)
	1381 ½ round face, smooth handles (circa 1879 to circa early 1920s)

1381 ½ flat face, chequered handles (circa early 1920s)

1382 Iron Spokeshave

Description

The 1382 and 1382½ spokeshaves are covered by U.S. patent 20,855, which was issued July 13, 1858 to Leonard Bailey of Winchester, Massachusetts. As this time, the term of a U.S. patent was 20 years from the earliest filing date or 17 years from the patent issue date, whichever is longer. As such, the earliest possible date that the Preston 1382 and 1382½ could have been produced without licensing Leonard Bailey's patent is July 13, 1875. The 1382 was likely discontinued when the 82 was introduced, most likely in the 1920s.

Dimensions

Length: 10 inches
Blade width: 2⅛ inches
Weight: 10 ¾ oz.

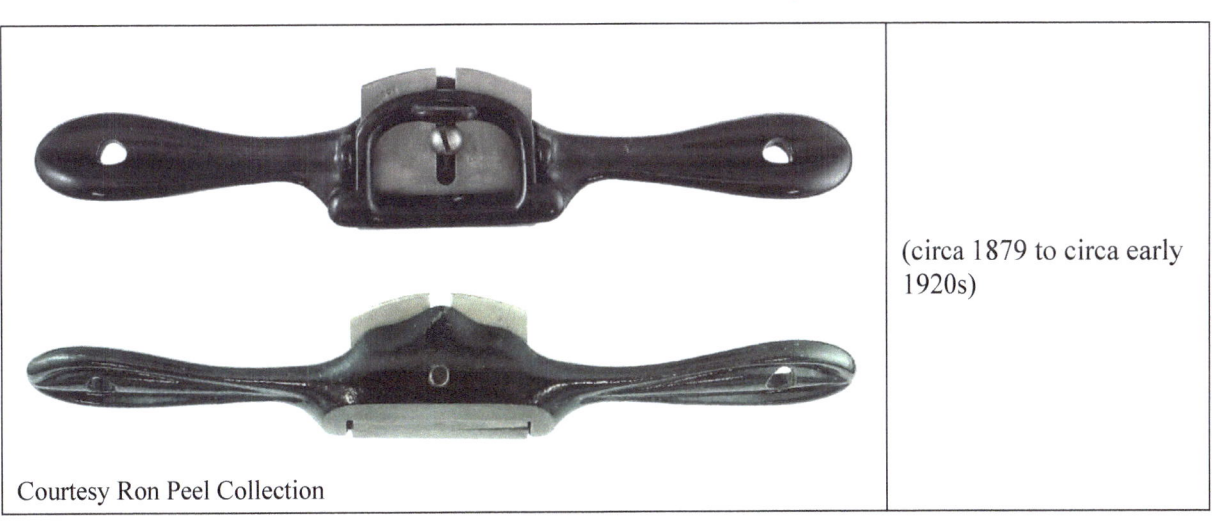

Courtesy Ron Peel Collection

(circa 1879 to circa early 1920s)

1382 ½ Iron Spokeshave

Description

The 1382 and 1382½ spokeshaves are covered by U.S. patent 20,855, which was issued July 13, 1858 to Leonard Bailey of Winchester, Massachusetts. As this time, the term of a U.S. patent was 20 years from the earliest filing date or 17 years from the patent issue date, whichever is longer. As such, the earliest possible date that the Preston 1382 and 1382½ could have been produced without licensing Leonard Bailey's patent is July 13, 1875. The 1382 ½ was likely discontinued when the 82 was introduced, most likely in the 1920s. On page 356 of *Manufactured and Patented Spokeshaves & Similar Tools* is a picture that is described as two versions of the 1382 ½ (similar to Stanley No. 53). The exact differences are not known to the author at this time.

Dimensions

Length: 9 ⅞ to 10 ¼ inches
Blade width: 2 ¹/₁₆ inches
Weight: 10 oz. to 10 ⅓ oz.

(circa 1879 to circa early 1920s)

1383 Iron Spokeshave

Description

The No. 1383 spokeshave was likely introduced around 1879. It appears to be a copy of Bailey's No. 5 spokeshave. This spokeshave was discontinued, most likely with the introduction of the No. 83 spokeshave in the 1920s.

Dimensions

Length: 9 $^{9}/_{16}$ inches
Blade width: 2 $^{1}/_{8}$ inches
Weight: 10 $^{2}/_{3}$ oz.

(circa 1879 to circa early 1920s)

1383 ½ Iron Spokeshave

Description

The No. 1383 ½ spokeshave was likely introduced around 1879. This spokeshave was discontinued, most likely in the 1920s.

Dimensions

Length: 10 inches
Blade width: 2 inches
Weight: 11 $^2/_3$ oz.

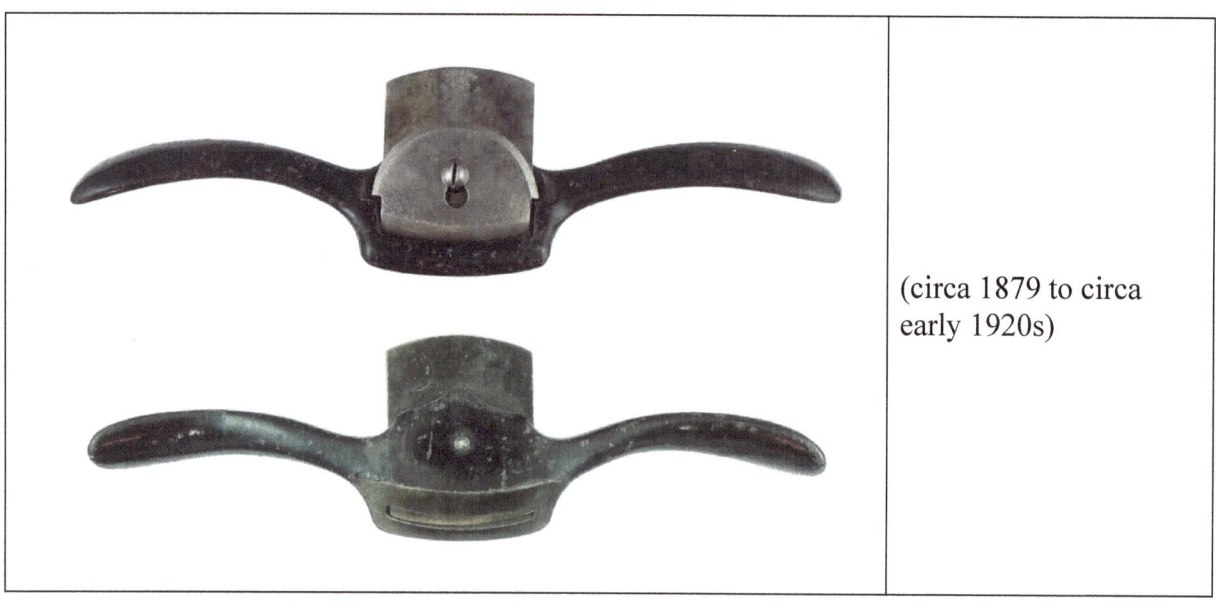

(circa 1879 to circa early 1920s)

1384 Iron Spokeshave

Description

The 1384 spokeshave is illustrated in an advertisement that appeared in the March 10, 1879 and March 15, 1879 *Australian and New Zealand Gazette*. This spokeshave was listed in the 1914 catalogue, but does not appear in either Price List No. 35 (1928) or Catalogue No. 43 (1932). At this time, it is not possible to provide a better estimate of when Preston stopped producing the 1384.

Dimensions

Length: 12 ½ inches
Blade width: 1 ³/₈ inches
Weight: 18 oz.

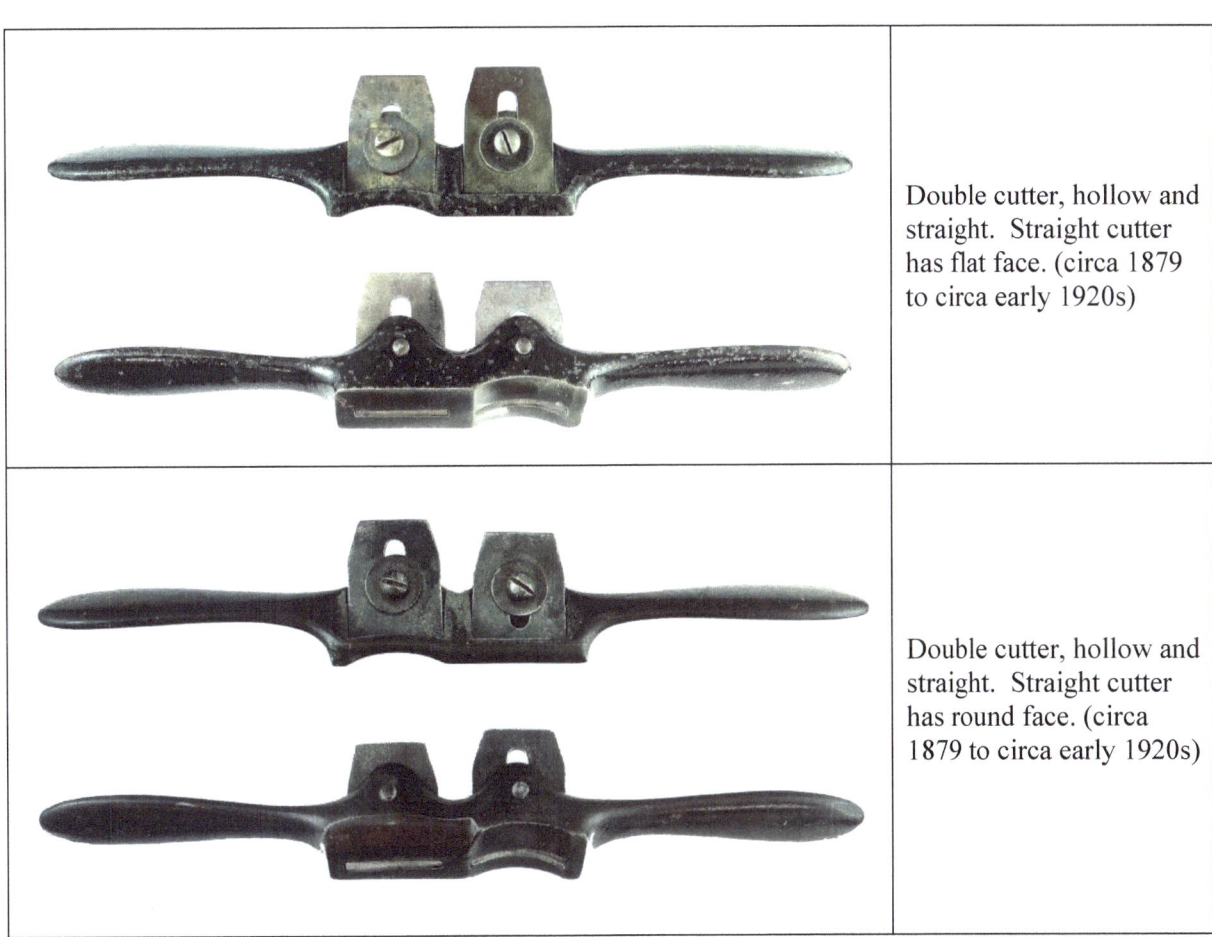

	Double cutter, hollow and straight. Straight cutter has flat face. (circa 1879 to circa early 1920s)
	Double cutter, hollow and straight. Straight cutter has round face. (circa 1879 to circa early 1920s)

1385 Improved Chamfer Shave

Description

The 1385 spokeshave is illustrated in an advertisement that appeared in the March 10, 1879 and March 15, 1879 *Australian and New Zealand Gazette*. This spokeshave was listed in the 1914 catalogue, but does not appear in either Price List No. 35 (1928) or Catalogue No. 43 (1932). At this time, it is not possible to provide a better estimate of when Preston stopped producing the 1385. All examples which have the Preston name stamped into the blades use ¼ inch BSW screws to fix the fences to the body of the spokeshave.

Dimensions

Length: 10 $^5/_{16}$ inches
Blade width: 1 $^3/_8$ inches
Weight: 16 $^2/_3$ oz.

Only one version of the Preston 1385 has been observed. There are similar spokeshaves with blades marked by other manufacturers. Please see the section on "Tools Manufactured for the Trade" (circa 1879 to late 1910s or early 1920s)

1386 Improved Circular Rabbeting and Fillister Router

Description

An Edward Preston advertisement published on October 1, 1880 mentions that Preston offers iron sash and rabbeting routers. As this is the only rabbeting router that Preston offered, Preston would have started its manufacture by 1880. The 1386 was supplied with 4 fences; however, it is commonly found with only the fence(s) that were used last by the craftsman.

Dimensions

Length: $11^{9}/_{16}$ inches
Blade width: $^{7}/_{8}$ inches
Weight: $20\,^{1}/_{2}$ oz. to $21\,^{1}/_{2}$ oz.

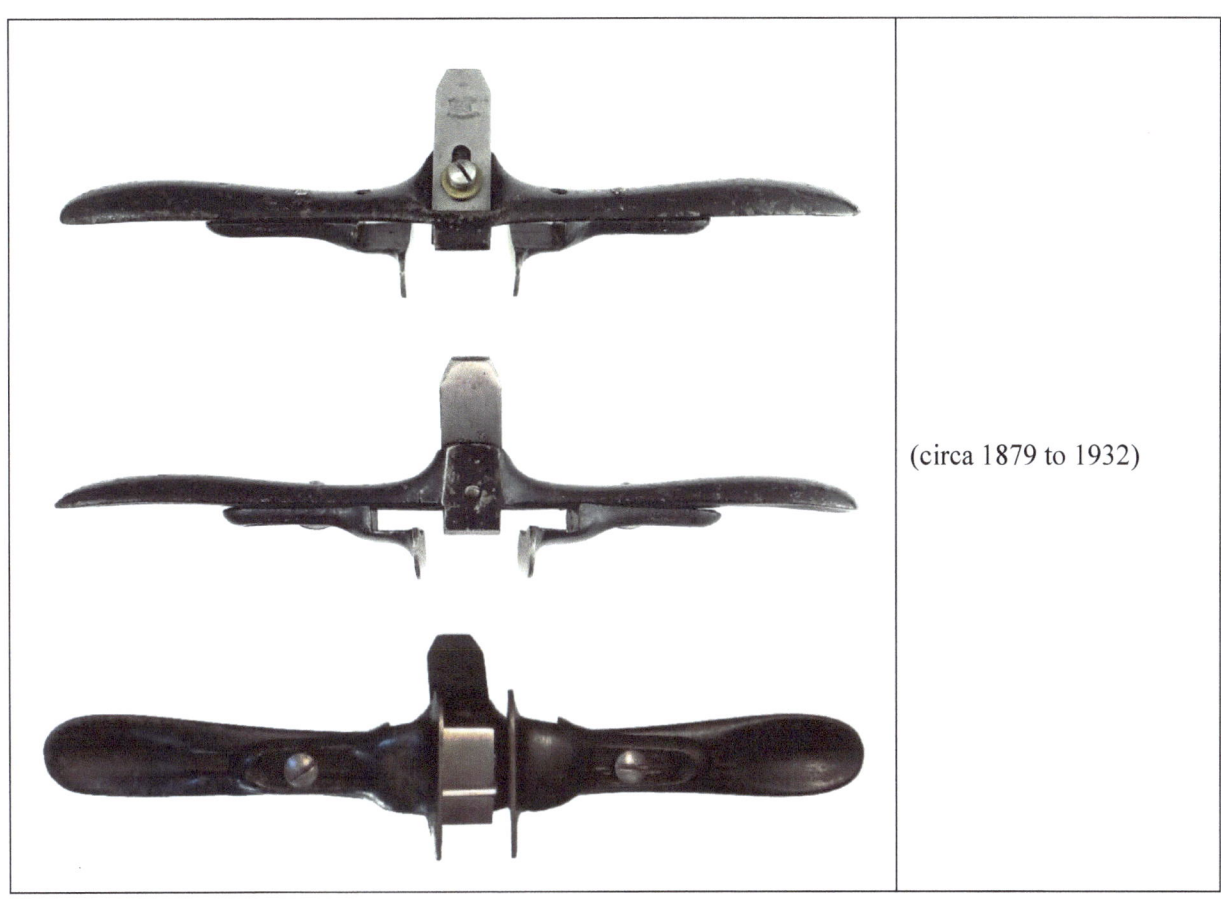

(circa 1879 to 1932)

On page 362 of *Manufactured and Patented Spokeshaves & Similar Tools* there is a picture that is described as circular rabbeting or fillister routers. The three tools in the picture appear to be of similar if not identical manufacture but are marked Preston, C & P Parks, and Marples, Hibernia. It is unknown if these were all manufactured by Preston or if these three companies made similar tools.

1387A Improved Circular Sash Router-Oveloe

Description

The sizes of 1387A improved circular sash router are listed in the Preston catalogues by the width of the glazing bar that the router is intended to cut. The catalogues list the sash planes with a combination of the width of the glazing bar as well as the depth. Observation of 1387A examples shows that the blades on some of these routers are marked with both dimensions while others are only marked with the width. An Edward Preston advertisement published on October 1, 1880 mentions that Preston offers iron sash and rabbeting routers. The 1387A sash router was listed in the 1932 Preston catalogue, indicating that it remained in production until Preston ceased trading.

Preston catalogues only listed these options for the 1387A:

- [ ] 1387A ½ inch Oveloe improved circular sash router
- [ ] 1387A $^9/_{16}$ inch Oveloe improved circular sash router
- [ ] 1387A ⅝ inch Oveloe improved circular sash router
- [ ] 1387A ¾ inch Oveloe improved circular sash router

Preston catalogues list the following Oveloe sash planes:

- [ ] ½ inch for 1 ½ inch bar
- [ ] $^9/_{16}$ inch for 1 ½ inch bar
- [ ] ⅝ inch for 1 ½ inch bar
- [ ] ⅝ inch for 1 ¾ inch bar
- [ ] ¾ inch for 1 ¾ inch bar

Dimensions

Length: 11 ½ inches to 11 ¾ inches
Blade width: 4 sizes were catalogued (½ inch to ¾ inch, with variations for bar size)
  Additional sizes have been observed, including $^3/_8$ inch
Weight: 13 $^2/_3$ oz. to 16 $^1/_3$ oz.

	1387A ³⁄₈ inch This size is not catalogued but several examples have been observed (circa 1880 to 1932)
	1387A ½ inch x 1 ½ inch (circa 1880 to 1932)
	1387A ⁹⁄₁₆ inch x 1 ½ inch (circa 1880 to 1932)
	1387A ⅝ inch x 1 ½ inch (circa 1880 to 1932)
	1387A ⅝ inch x 1 ¾ inch (circa 1880 to 1932)

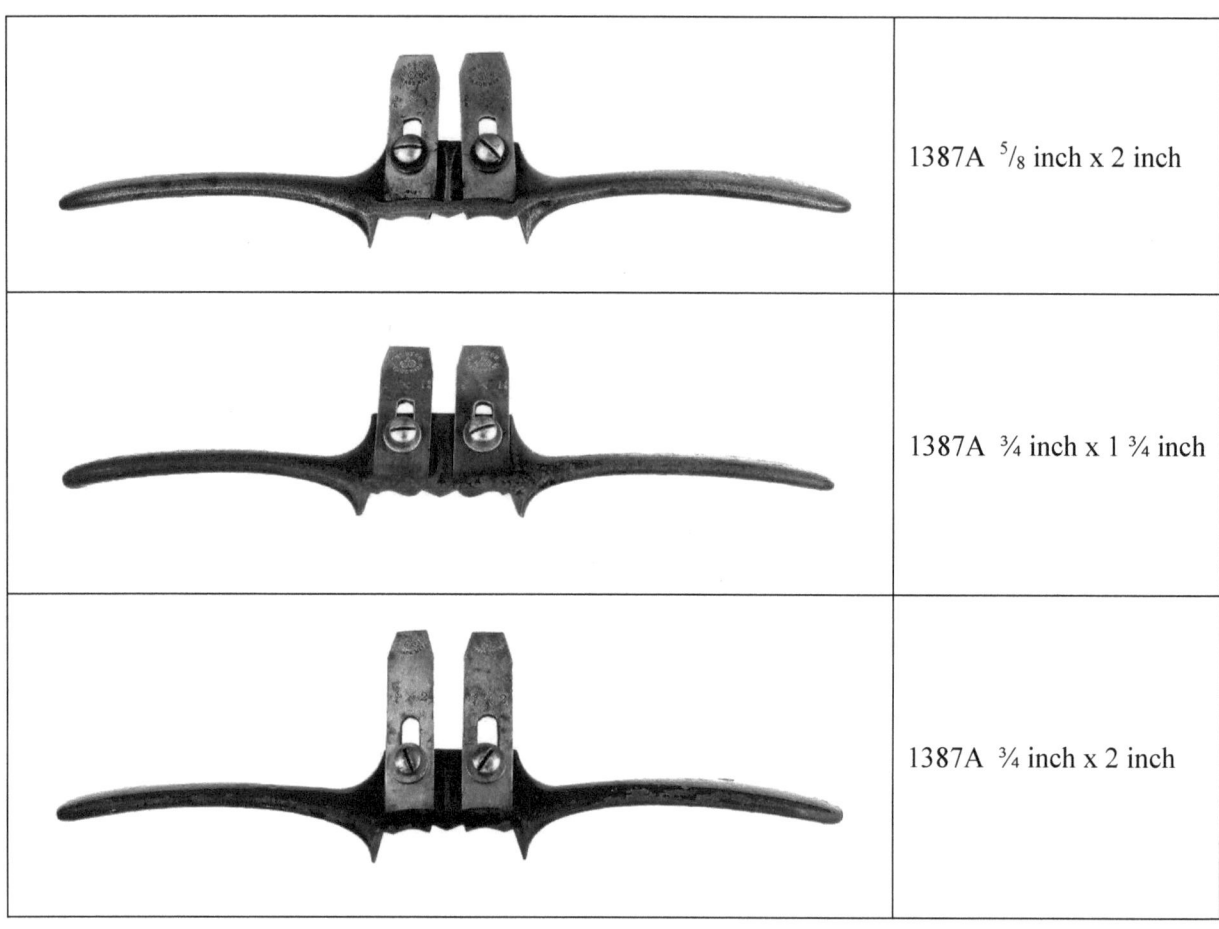	1387A ⁵⁄₈ inch x 2 inch
	1387A ¾ inch x 1 ¾ inch
	1387A ¾ inch x 2 inch

1387B Improved Circular Sash Router – Lamb Tongue

Description

The sizes of 1387B improved circular sash router are listed in the Preston catalogues by the width of the glazing bar that the router is intended to cut. The catalogues list the sash planes with a combination of the width of the glazing bar as well as the depth (size of bar). Observation of 1387B examples shows that the blades on some of these routers are marked with both dimensions while others are only marked with the width. An Edward Preston advertisement published on October 1, 1880 mentions that Preston offers iron sash and rabbeting routers. The 1387B was discontinued sometime after 1928 and prior to 1932.

Preston catalogues only listed these options for the 1387B:
- ☐ 1387B ½ inch Lamb Tongue improved circular sash router
- ☐ 1387B $9/16$ inch Lamb Tongue improved circular sash router
- ☐ 1387B ⅝ inch Lamb Tongue improved circular sash router
- ☐ 1387B ¾ inch Lamb Tongue improved circular sash router

Preston catalogues list the following Lamb Tongue sash planes:
- ☐ ½ inch for 1 ½ inch bar
- ☐ $9/16$ inch for 1 ½ inch bar
- ☐ ⅝ inch for 1 ¾ inch bar
- ☐ ⅝ inch for 2 inch bar
- ☐ ¾ inch for 2 inch bar

Dimensions

Length: 11 ⅜ inches to 12 inches
Blade width: 4 sizes were catalogued (½ inch to ¾ inch, with variations for bar size)
Weight: 13 ½ oz. to 18 ¾ oz.

	1387B ½ inch (introduced circa 1880 and withdrawn between 1928 and 1932)
Picture Not Available	1387B ⁹/₁₆ inch (introduced circa 1880 and withdrawn between 1928 and 1932)
	1387B ⅝ inch x 1 ½ inch (introduced circa 1880 and withdrawn between 1928 and 1932)
	1387B ⅝ inch x 1 ¾ inch (introduced circa 1880 and withdrawn between 1928 and 1932)
	1387B ⅝ inch likely x 2 inch (introduced circa 1880 and withdrawn between 1928 and 1932)
	1387B ¾ inch x 2 inch (introduced circa 1880 and withdrawn between 1928 and 1932)

1387C Improved Circular Sash Router – Gothic

Description

The sizes of 1387C improved circular sash router are listed in the Preston catalogues by the width of the glazing bar that the router is intended to cut. The catalogues list the sash planes with a combination of the width of the glazing bar as well as the depth. Observation of 1387C examples shows that the blades on some of these routers are marked with both dimensions while others are only marked with the width. An Edward Preston advertisement published on October 1, 1880 mentions that Preston offers iron sash and rabbeting routers. The 1387C was discontinued sometime after 1928 and prior to 1932.

Preston catalogues only listed these options for the 1387C:

- ☐ 1387C ½ inch Gothic improved circular sash router
- ☐ 1387C $^9/_{16}$ inch Gothic improved circular sash router
- ☐ 1387C ⅝ inch Gothic improved circular sash router
- ☐ 1387C ¾ inch Gothic improved circular sash router

Preston catalogues list the following Gothic sash planes:

- ☐ ½ inch for 1 ½ inch bar
- ☐ $^9/_{16}$ inch for 1 ½ inch bar
- ☐ ⅝ inch for 1 ¾ inch bar
- ☐ ⅝ inch for 2 inch bar
- ☐ ¾ inch for 2 inch bar

Dimensions

Length: 11 ¾ inches to 11 ⅞ inches
Blade width: 4 sizes were catalogued (½ inch to ¾ inch, with variations for bar size)
Weight: 16 oz. to 17 oz.

Picture Not Available	1387C ½ inch
	1387C ⁹⁄₁₆ inch (introduced circa 1880 and withdrawn between 1928 and 1932)
	1387C ⅝ inch x 2 inch (introduced circa 1880 and withdrawn between 1928 and 1932)
	1387 C ¾ inch likely x 1¾ inch (introduced circa 1880 and withdrawn between 1928 and 1932)
	1387 C ¾ inch likely x 2 inch (introduced circa 1880 and withdrawn between 1928 and 1932)

1387D Improved Circular Common Oveloe Router

Description

Some examples of the 1387D have C.O. (for Common Oveloe) cast into the handle next to the size. The 1387D was introduced between 1901 and 1909. The 1387D was listed in *Preston Catalogue No. 43* (1932) but not in *John Rabone & Sons Catalogue No. 27* (1933).

Dimensions

Length: 11 ½ inches to 12 inches
Blade width: 5 sizes were catalogued (¼ inch to ¾ inch)
Weight: 16 ⅞ oz.

Picture Not Available	1387D ¼ inch improved circular common oveloe router. (introduced between 1901 and 1909, available to 1932)
	1387D ⅜ inch improved circular common oveloe router. (introduced between 1901 and 1909, available to 1932)
Picture Not Available	1387D ½ inch improved circular common oveloe router. (introduced between 1901 and 1909, available to 1932)
	1387D ⅝ inch improved circular common oveloe router. (introduced between 1901 and 1909, available to 1932)
	1387D ¾ inch improved circular common oveloe router.(introduced between 1901 and 1909, available to 1932)

1387E Improved Circular Equal or Square Oveloe Router

Description

Some examples have the size and the letters "SO" (for Square Oveloe) cast into the underside of the handle. Some examples have the size and the letters "SO" (for Square Oveloe) cast into the underside of the handle. The 1387E was introduced between 1901 and 1909. The 1387E was listed in *Preston Catalogue No. 43* (1932) but not in *John Rabone & Sons Catalogue No. 27* (1933).

Dimensions

Length: 11 $^{3}/_{8}$ inches to 12 inches
Blade width: 5 sizes were catalogued (¼ x ¼ inch to ¾ x ¾ inch)
Weight: 14 $^{3}/_{4}$ oz. to 20 oz.

Picture Not Available	1387E ¼ x ¼ inch improved circular equal or square oveloe router (introduced between 1901 and 1909, available to 1932)
Picture Not Available	1387E ⅜ x ⅜ inch improved circular equal or square oveloe router (introduced between 1901 and 1909, available to 1932)
	1387E ½ x ½ inch improved circular equal or square oveloe router. (introduced between 1901 and 1909, available to 1932)
	1387E $^{9}/_{16}$ x $^{9}/_{16}$ inch improved circular equal or square oveloe router. (introduced between 1901 and 1909, available to 1932)

	1387E ⅝ x ⅝ inch improved circular equal or square oveloe router. (introduced between 1901 and 1909, available to 1932)
	1387E ¾ x ¾ inch improved circular equal or square oveloe router (introduced between 1901 and 1909, available to 1932)

1388 Improved Circular Quirk or Grooving Router

Description

The 1388 quirk router was provided with three blades and three fences. The 1388 does not have the depth adjuster that is found on the 1388P. The first known catalogue listing of the No. 1388 was found in the 1885 Richard Melhuish catalogue. This indicates that the 1388 was available for over 40 years. The model 1388 quirk router was listed in the 1933 John Rabone & Sons catalogue. The Rabone catalogue indicated that Rabone had purchased Preston.

Dimensions

Length: 12 ½ inches to 12 ⅞ inches
Blade width: various interchangeable blade widths ($^3/_{32}$ inch to $^3/_{16}$ inch)
Weight: 26 ⅞ oz. (With 3 fences and 2 blades)

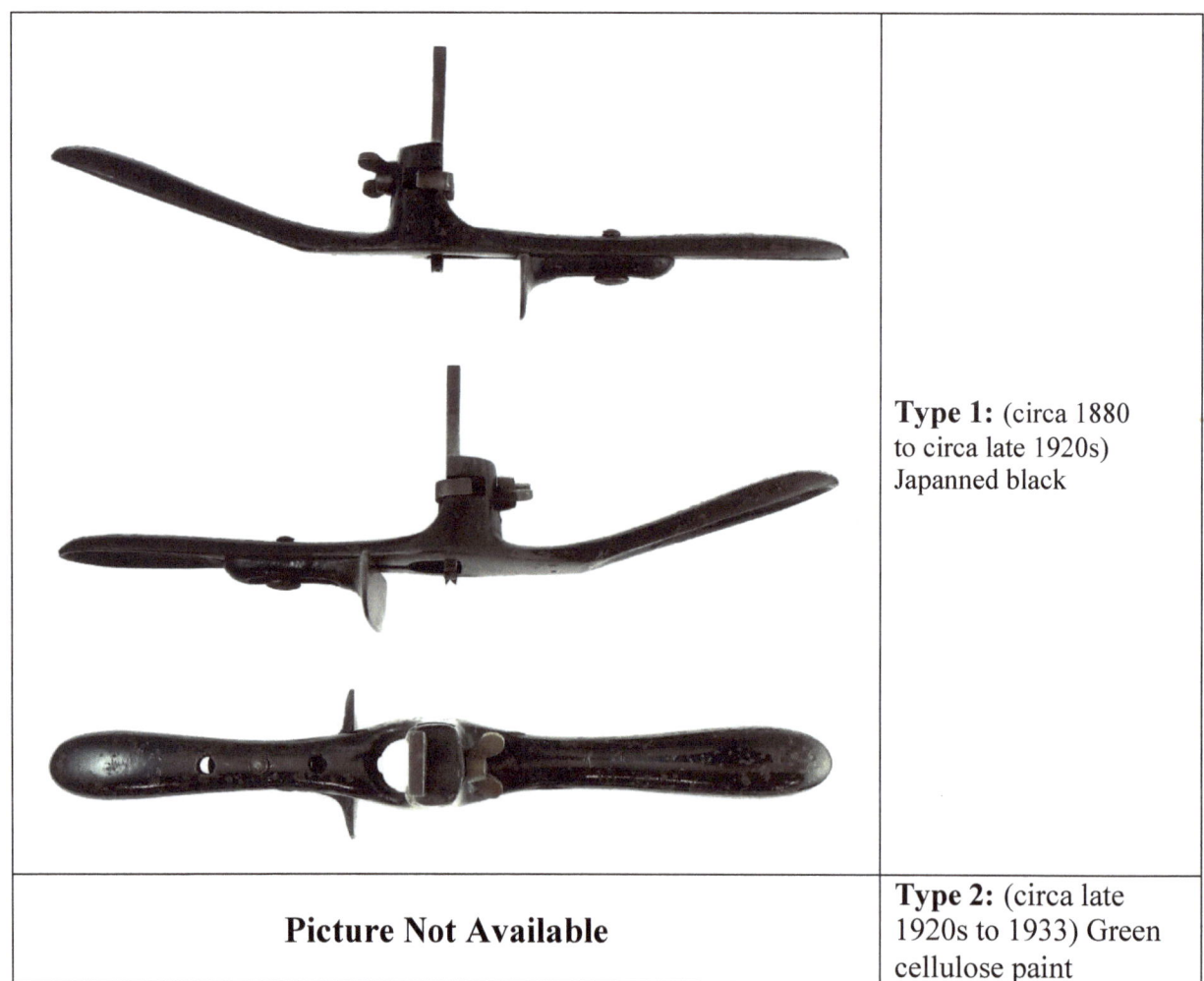

	Type 1: (circa 1880 to circa late 1920s) Japanned black
Picture Not Available	**Type 2:** (circa late 1920s to 1933) Green cellulose paint

Blades

The 1388 was supplied with 3 blades: $^3/_{32}$ inch, $^1/_8$ inch, and $^3/_{16}$ inch. The blades for the 1388 can be distinguished from 1388P blades in that they lack the slot for the adjustment screw on the 1388P. The blades from a 1388P can be used in a 1388, but 1388 blades cannot be used in a 1388P.

Left: 1388 blade without slot

Right: 1388P blade with slot for adjustment screw

Fences

The 1388 was supplied with 3 fences.

1388P Patent Adjustable Circular Quirk or Grooving Router

Description

The 1388P quirk router was provided with three blades and three fences. The 1388P is similar to the 1388 with the addition of a depth adjuster. The 1388P was listed in the 1895 through 1932 editions of the Preston catalogue. The 1388P was introduced after the 1891 Preston Catalogue was issued.

Dimensions

Length: 12½ inches to 12⅝ inches
Blade width: various interchangeable blade widths (³/₃₂ inch to ³/₁₆ inch)
Weight: 23 ⅓ oz.

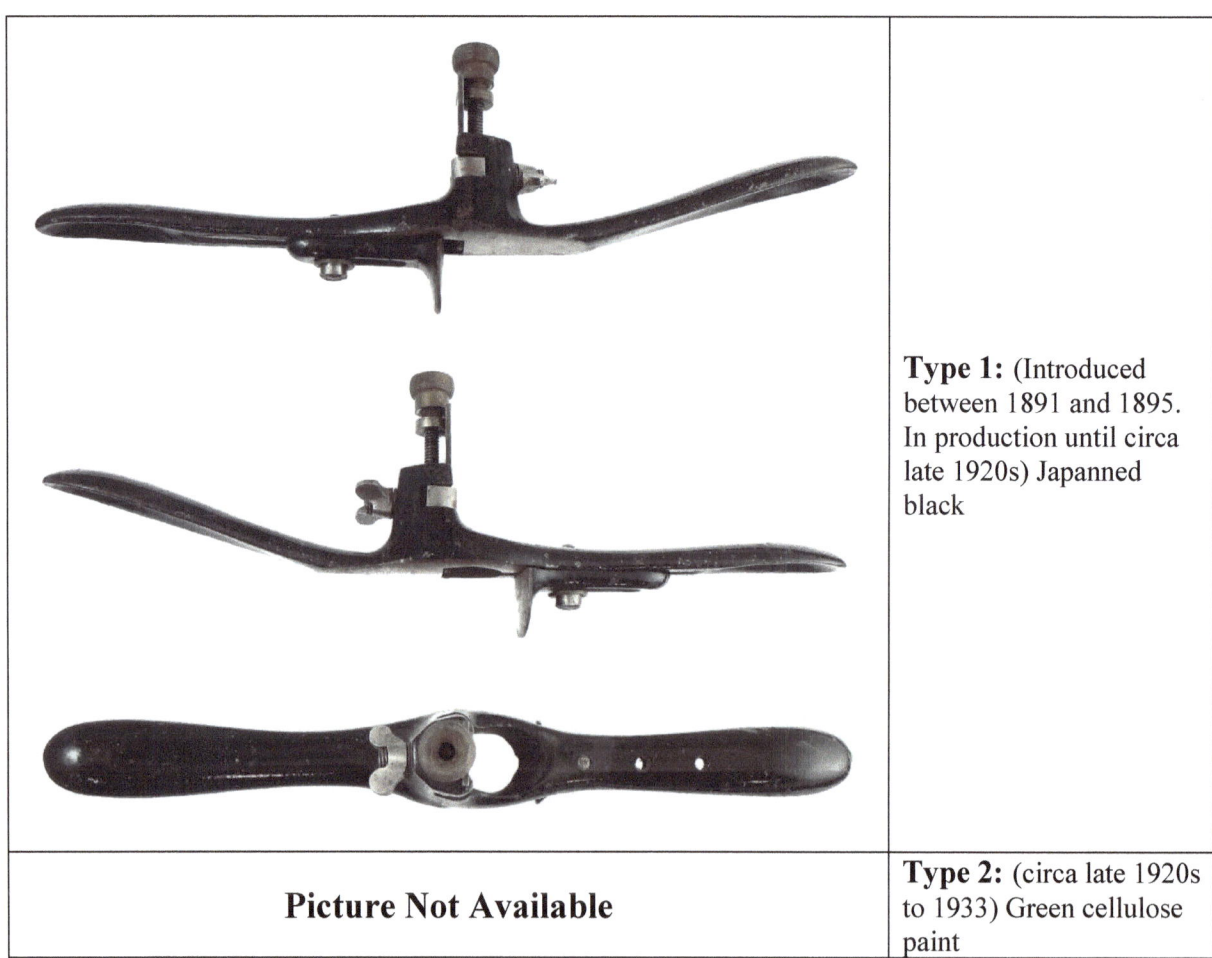

	Type 1: (Introduced between 1891 and 1895. In production until circa late 1920s) Japanned black
Picture Not Available	**Type 2:** (circa late 1920s to 1933) Green cellulose paint

Blades

The 1388P was supplied with 3 blades: $^3/_{32}$ inch, $^1/_8$ inch, and $^3/_{16}$ inch The blades for the 1388 can be distinguished from 1388P blades in that they lack the slot for the adjustment screw on the 1388P. The blades from a 1388P can be used in a 1388, but 1388 blades cannot be used in a 1388P.

Left: 1388 blade without slot

Right: 1388P blade with slot for adjustment screw

Fences

The 1388P was supplied with 3 fences.

1389 Improved Circular Bead Router

Description

Circular bead routers are used in conjunction with side bead planes. Side bead planes will put a bead on the straight side of a board, but are not capable of working on curved surfaces. The short sole of a circular bead router allows a craftsman to work a bead on a curved surface and although a bead router can be used on a straight section of wood, using a side bead plane is easier. The 1389 bead routers were introduced prior to 1886 and remained in production until 1932.

Dimensions

Length: $11 \frac{1}{8}$ inches to $11 \frac{7}{8}$ inches
Blade width: 12 sizes ranging from $\frac{1}{8}$ inch to 1 inch
Weight: 12 oz. to $16 \frac{3}{4}$ oz.

	1389 $\frac{1}{8}$ inch bead (prior to 1886 to 1932)
Picture Not Available	1389 $\frac{3}{16}$ inch bead (prior to 1886 to 1932)
	1389 ¼ inch bead (prior to 1886 to 1932)
	1389 $\frac{5}{16}$ inch bead (prior to 1886 to 1932)

	1389 3/8 inch bead (prior to 1886 to 1932)
	1389 7/16 inch bead (prior to 1886 to 1932)
	1389 ½ inch bead (prior to 1886 to 1932)
	1389 9/16 inch bead (prior to 1886 to 1932)
	1389 5/8 inch bead (prior to 1886 to 1932)

	1389 ¾ inch bead (prior to 1886 to 1932)
	1389 ⅞ inch bead (prior to 1886 to 1932)
Picture Not Available	1389 1 inch bead (prior to 1886 to 1932)

1390 Patent Iron Spokeshave

Description

The 1390 spokeshave was illustrated in the 1891, 1895, and 1901 catalogues but not in the 1909 catalogue. The 1909 catalogue did have a listing which indicated that the 1390 was similar to the 1390H except with solid handles. The 1390 is not listed in the Booklet No. 23 (circa 1911) or the 1914 catalogue. The 1390 seems to be less common that the 1390H. The 1390 may have been produced as early as 1886 and production was stopped sometime between 1909 and 1912.

Dimensions

Length: 9 $^7/_8$ inches
Blade width: 2 inches
Weight: 10 oz.

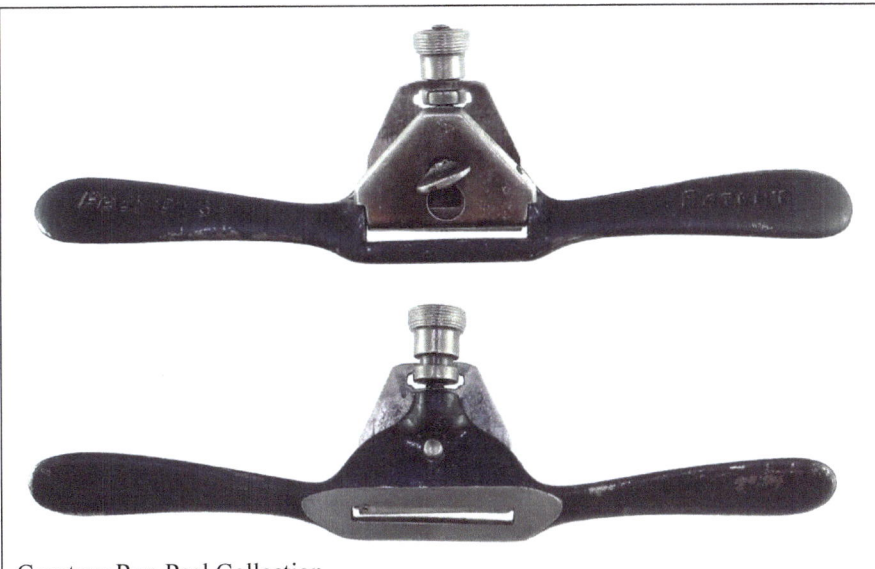

Courtesy Ron Peel Collection

Type 1 with straight handles. Marked PRESTONS PATENT with smooth top plate. It appears that Preston made a straight handled version and a raised handle version as was done for the 1381 and 1382. The casting behind the blade is different from the raised handle version. Note: This example has a blade that is meant for a spokeshave with a lateral adjuster.

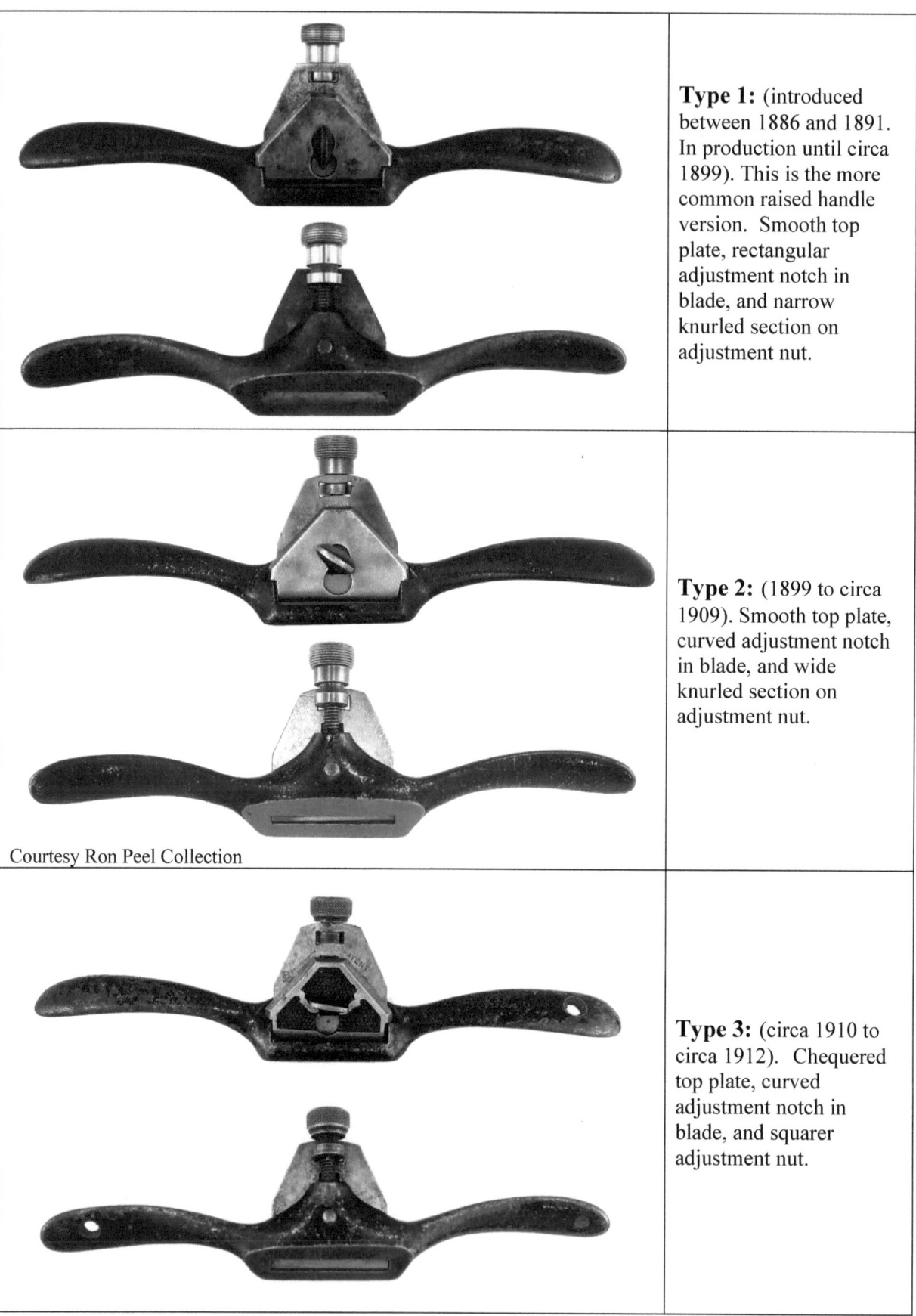

Type 1: (introduced between 1886 and 1891. In production until circa 1899). This is the more common raised handle version. Smooth top plate, rectangular adjustment notch in blade, and narrow knurled section on adjustment nut.

Type 2: (1899 to circa 1909). Smooth top plate, curved adjustment notch in blade, and wide knurled section on adjustment nut.

Courtesy Ron Peel Collection

Type 3: (circa 1910 to circa 1912). Chequered top plate, curved adjustment notch in blade, and squarer adjustment nut.

1390H Patent Iron Spokeshave

Description

The 1390H is a commonly found spokeshave. The 1390H was listed in the 1891 Preston catalogue. The first versions of the 1390H have no identifying marks on the main casting or top plate. The only markings appear on the blade. Starting with catalogue No. 26 (May 1914), the 1390H is depicted as being a japanned spokeshave with the ornate body as seen on the 1391. The lateral adjuster is introduced in the 1914 catalogue. Preston used different model numbers for japanned and nickel plated versions of the spokeshave. The 1390H was available with either a flat face or round face.

Please see the entry for the 2501 for the spokeshave that looks like the early 1390H with offset handles. This spokeshave is incorrectly identified as the 1390H with offset handles in other publications, most likely due to the scarcity of Preston catalogues.

Dimensions

Length: 9 $\frac{7}{8}$ inches to 10 $\frac{1}{8}$ inches
Blade width: 2 inches
Weight: 10 $\frac{1}{2}$ oz. to 12 oz.

Type 1 illustration used in 1892 Richard Melhuish Catalogue, 1901 Preston Catalogue, and 1909 Preston Catalogue

This drawing illustrates the working method of the adjustment to the Cutting Irons and shews clearly the Wing Adjuster for adjusting the Iron laterally or sideways.

No. 1390H.   Hollow Raised Handles, Japanned, 10 inches, Flat face, 2 inch Cutting Iron ... ... 2/6 each.

No. 1390H. R.F. Hollow Raised Handles, Japanned, 10 inches, Round face, 2 inch Cutting Iron ... ... 2/6 each.

1914 Preston catalogue entry introducing the lateral adjuster and ornate main casting (type 6).

Type 1: (introduced between 1886 and 1891. In production until circa 1899). Japanned, plain body, no lateral adjuster, and smooth top plate. This type has a narrow knurled section on the adjustment nut and the slot in the blade is rectangular in shape.

Type 2: (1899 to circa 1909). Japanned, plain body, no lateral adjuster, and smooth top plate. The adjustment slot in the blade is now curved per patent number 15,549. The knurled section of the adjustment nut is now wider.

Type 3: (circa 1910 to circa 1913). Japanned, plain body, no lateral adjuster, and chequered top plate

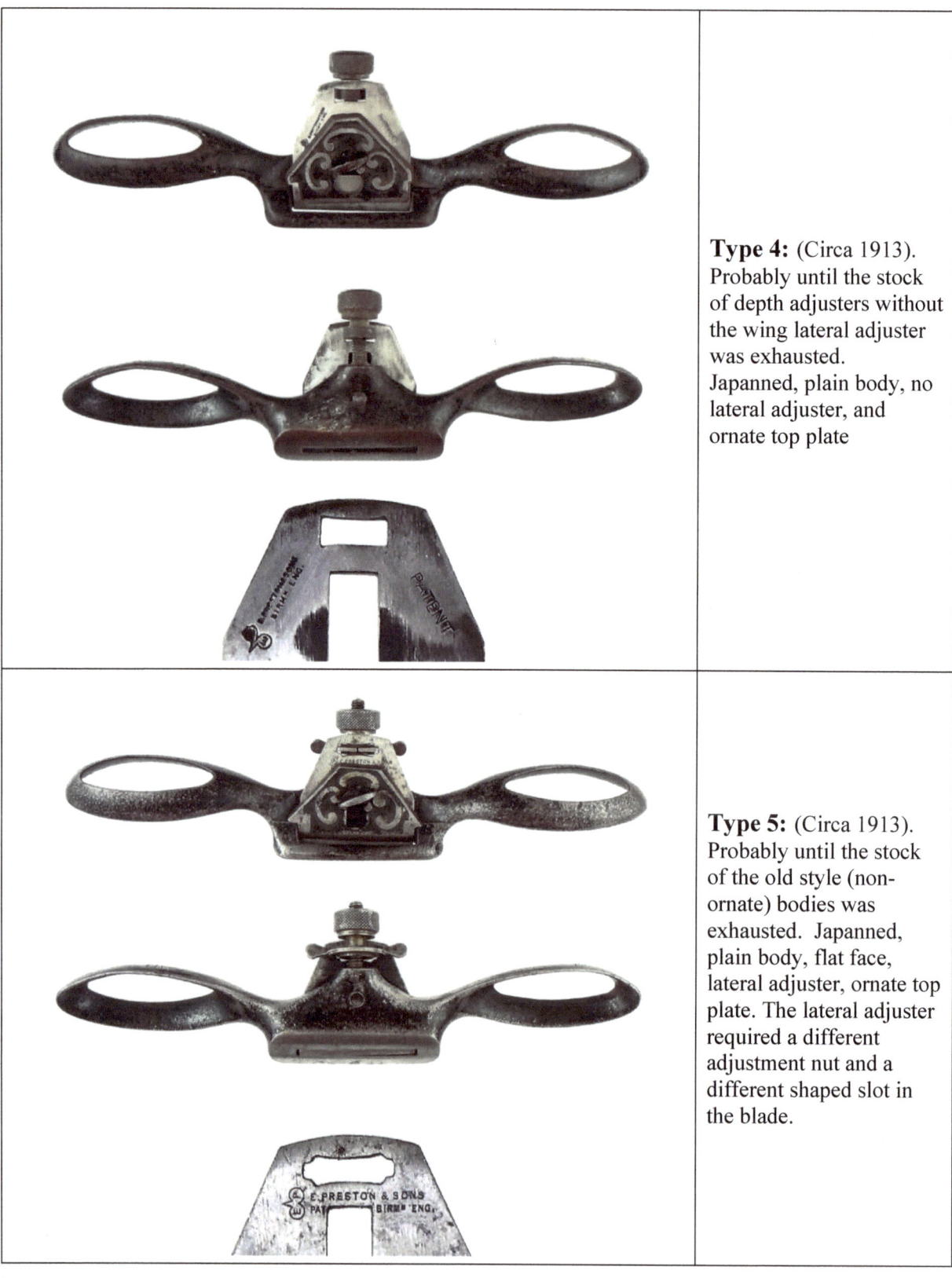

Type 4: (Circa 1913). Probably until the stock of depth adjusters without the wing lateral adjuster was exhausted. Japanned, plain body, no lateral adjuster, and ornate top plate

Type 5: (Circa 1913). Probably until the stock of the old style (non-ornate) bodies was exhausted. Japanned, plain body, flat face, lateral adjuster, ornate top plate. The lateral adjuster required a different adjustment nut and a different shaped slot in the blade.

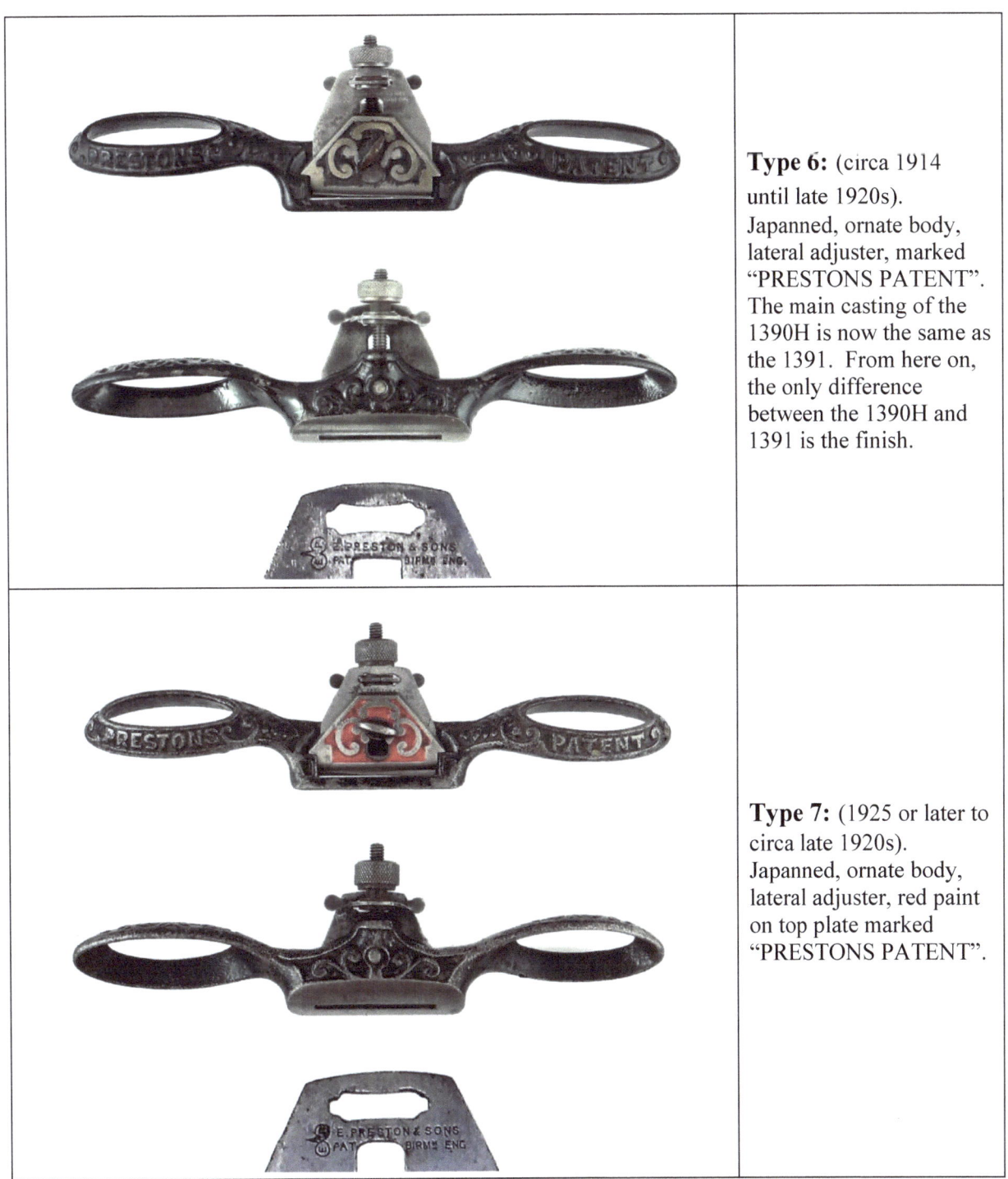

Type 6: (circa 1914 until late 1920s). Japanned, ornate body, lateral adjuster, marked "PRESTONS PATENT". The main casting of the 1390H is now the same as the 1391. From here on, the only difference between the 1390H and 1391 is the finish.

Type 7: (1925 or later to circa late 1920s). Japanned, ornate body, lateral adjuster, red paint on top plate marked "PRESTONS PATENT".

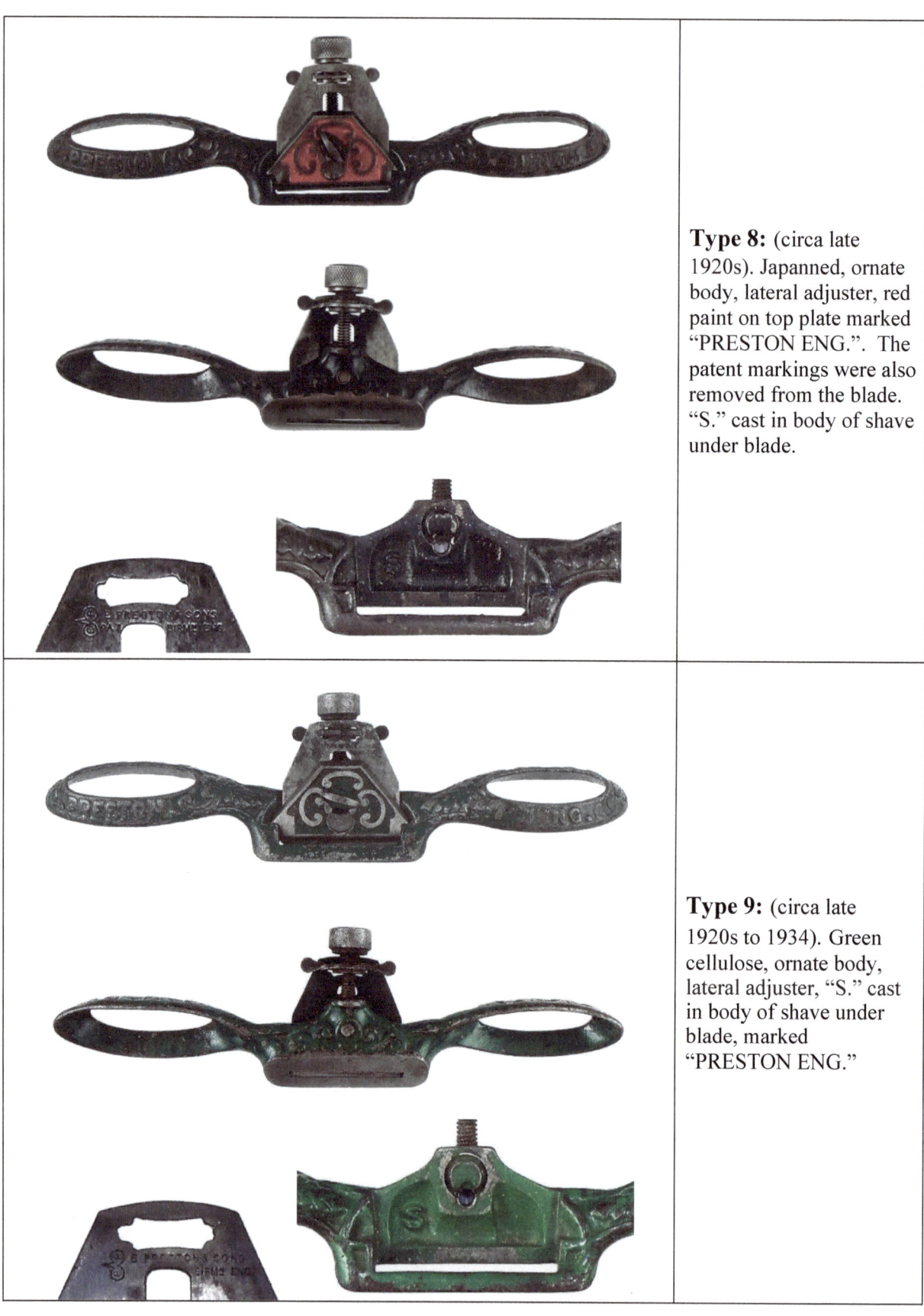

Type 8: (circa late 1920s). Japanned, ornate body, lateral adjuster, red paint on top plate marked "PRESTON ENG.". The patent markings were also removed from the blade. "S." cast in body of shave under blade.

Type 9: (circa late 1920s to 1934). Green cellulose, ornate body, lateral adjuster, "S." cast in body of shave under blade, marked "PRESTON ENG."

1391 Patent Iron Spokeshave

Description

The 1391 is a very ornate, nickel plated spokeshave that was produced from 1898 until Preston ceased trading in 1932.

The 1914 Preston catalogue shows the 1391 with the lateral adjuster. The 1914 catalogue additionally shows that the 1391 is only available nickel plated and that the same casting was available with a japanned finish and sold as the 1390H. The 1391 is available with either round or flat faces in all of these catalogues. The depth adjuster on the spokeshaves marked "Preston. Eng." has a deep, square bottomed hollow in the top. The other spokeshaves with the lateral adjuster have a shallow conical hollow in the top. The spokeshaves marked "Preston. Eng." seem to have blades where the marking "Pat" or "Patent" has been removed.

Dimensions

Length: 9 $^{11}/_{16}$ inches to 10 $^{1}/_{8}$ inches
Blade width: 2 inches
Weight: 9 $^{2}/_{3}$ oz. to 11 $^{7}/_{8}$ oz.

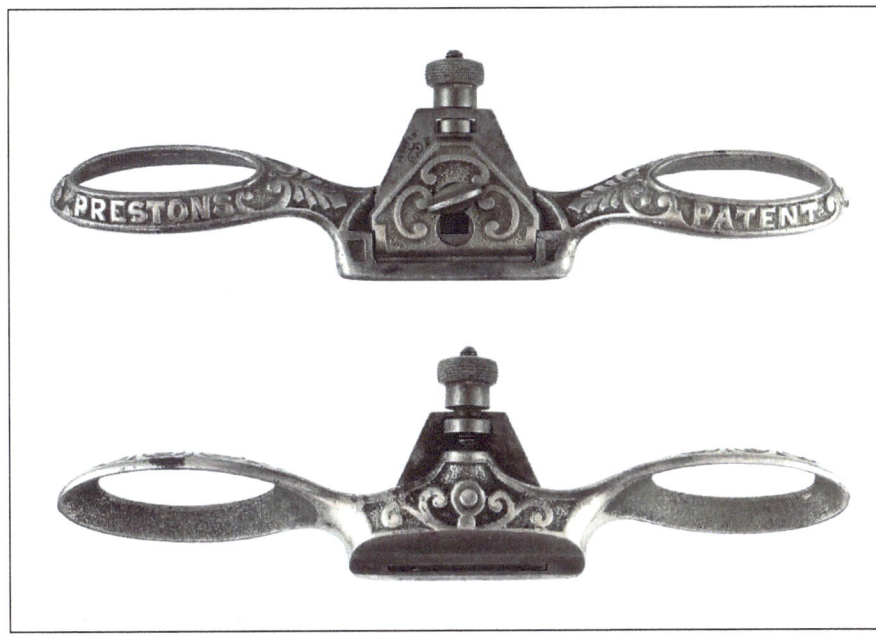

Type 1: (circa 1898). Nickel plated, no lateral adjuster, and marked "PRESTONS PATENT"

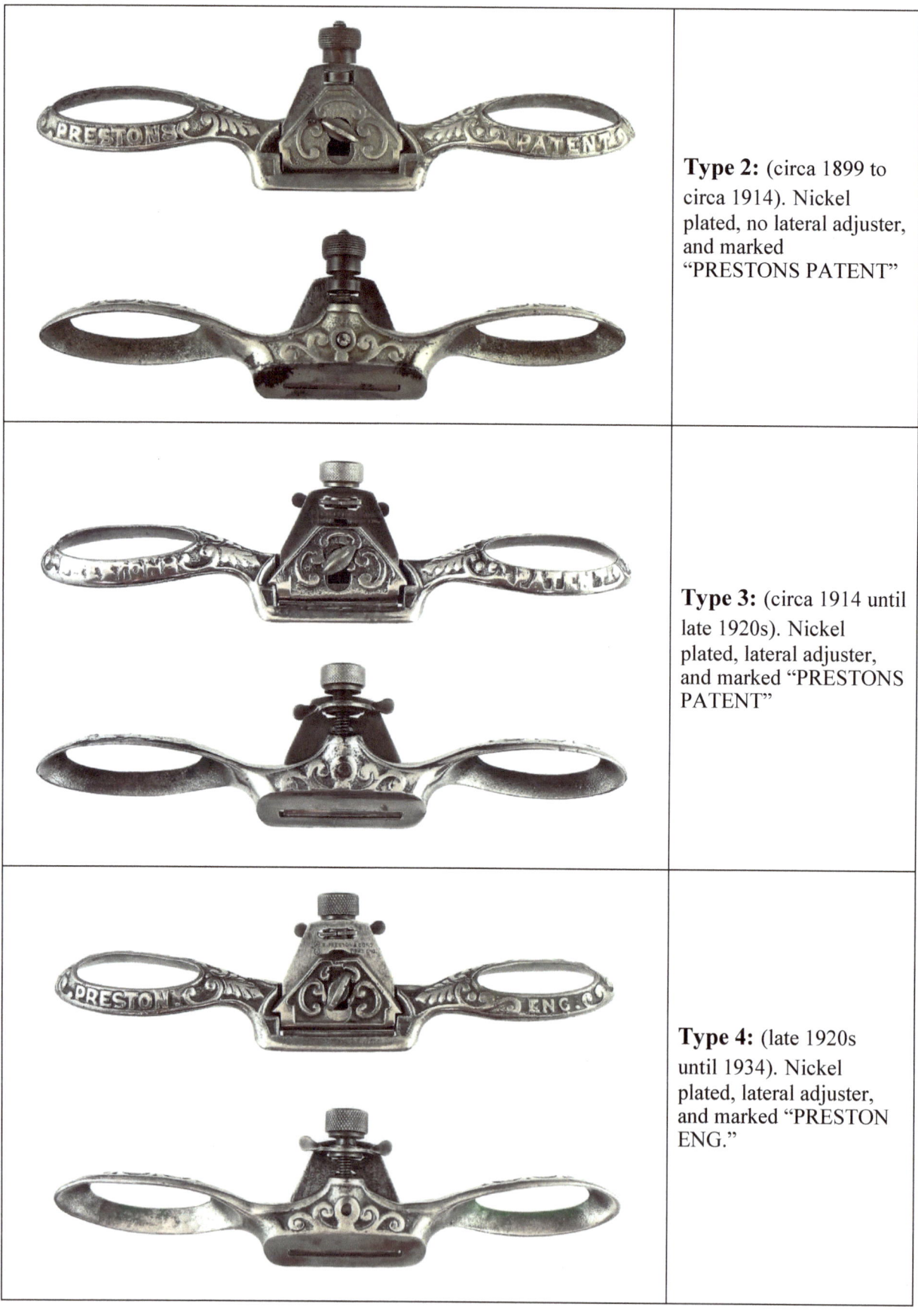

Type 2: (circa 1899 to circa 1914). Nickel plated, no lateral adjuster, and marked "PRESTONS PATENT"

Type 3: (circa 1914 until late 1920s). Nickel plated, lateral adjuster, and marked "PRESTONS PATENT"

Type 4: (late 1920s until 1934). Nickel plated, lateral adjuster, and marked "PRESTON ENG."

1392 Patent Adjustable Stop Chamfer Shave

Description

The 1392 Patent adjustable stop spokeshave was announced in the January 1, 1886 edition of *The British Trade Journal*. The patent for the depth adjuster was applied for on October 19, 1885. The smooth top plate is illustrated in *Preston Catalogue No. 18* (1909). The Chequered top plate with lateral adjuster is illustrated in *Preston Catalogue No. 26* (1914). The 1392 remained in production until Preston ceased trading in 1932.

IMPROVED CARPENTERS' TOOLS.

We here illustrate a new patent adjustable-stop chamfer-shave, which, among other improved carpenters' and joiners' tools, has recently been brought out by Messrs. Edward Preston & Sons, of Whittal Works, Birmingham. The first sketch shows a front and the second a back view of the new

tool. The cutting-iron, it will be seen, is adjusted by a milled nut, instead of by the hammer. A few turns of the nut will give any cut desired much more quickly and certainly than the repeated blows of the hammer applied in the old tools.

As the tool makes its own "stop" the use of the chisel is dispensed with, the chamfer and "stop" being made at the same time. The top-plate of the cutting-iron and the fences can be adjusted and fixed by the three thumbscrews shown in the first sketch. A turn-screw or screw-driver of any kind can, therefore, be dispensed with in using this tool, which also possesses other advantages, adding to the efficiency, rapidity, and nicety with which work of this class can be done.

Announcement from January 1, 1886 edition of *The British Trade Journal*

Dimensions

Length: 10 ¼ inches to 10 ⁵⁄₁₆ inches
Blade width: 1¾ inches
Weight: 13 ¾ oz. without lateral adjuster
15 ¼ oz. with lateral adjuster

Type 1: (circa 1885 to circa late 1880s) Note the taper to the depth adjustment nut and the short fences which match the 1885 patent application illustration.

Type 2: (circa late 1880's to circa 1908). The fences are now long. The long fences were shown in the 1891 Preston catalogue.

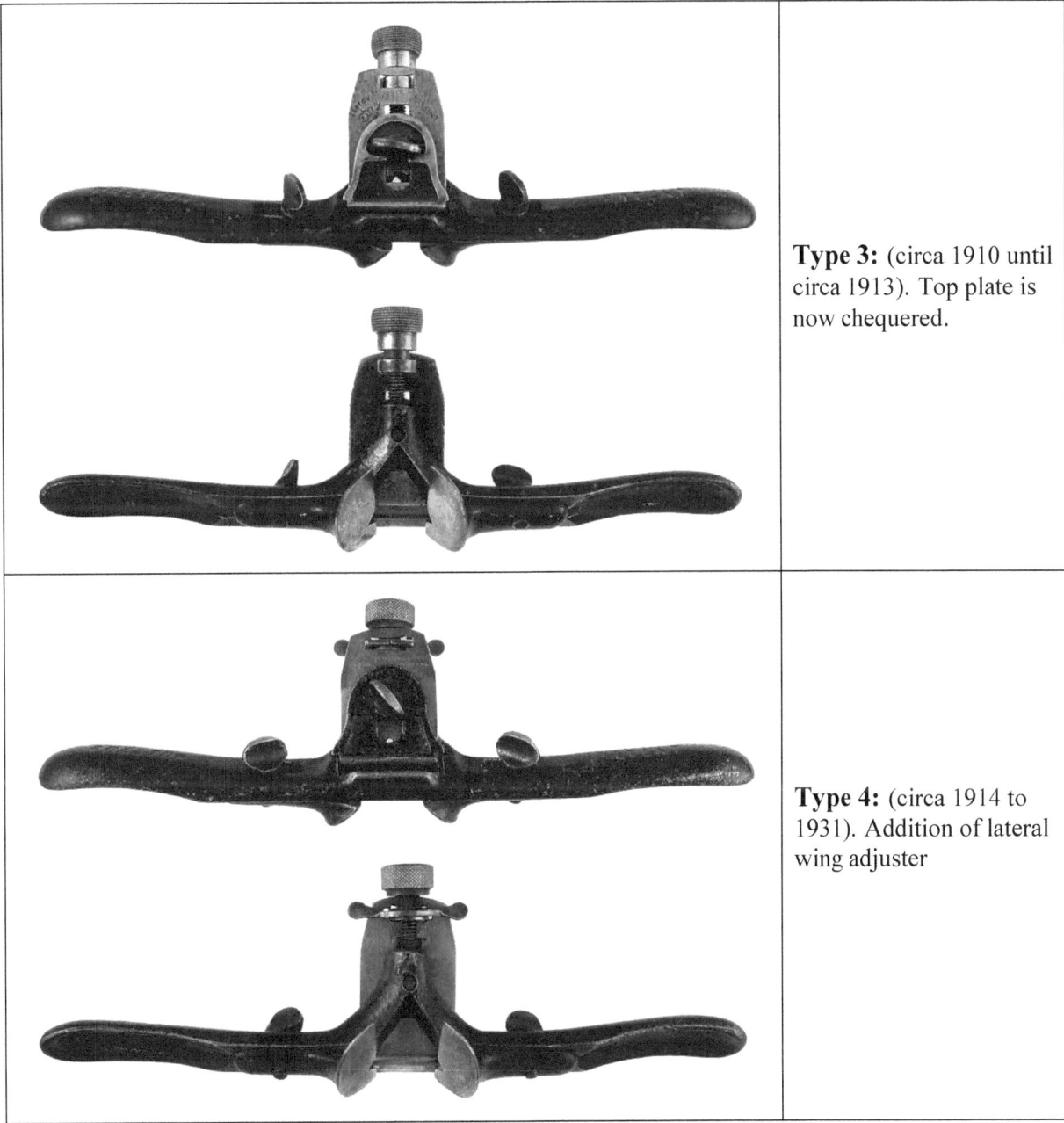

Type 3: (circa 1910 until circa 1913). Top plate is now chequered.

Type 4: (circa 1914 to 1931). Addition of lateral wing adjuster

1393 Patent Hand Reeder and Moulding Tool

Description

The lever cap for this tool is covered by patent 8296, issued in 1886. The 1393 Patent hand reeder is shown in the 1889-1890 Birmingham directory. It appears in the 1891 through 1932 editions of the Preston catalogue. A version with green cellulose paint is suspected, but has never been observed by the author.

Dimensions

Length: 13 ¼ inches
Blade width: ³/₄ and 1¼ inch wide interchangeable blades
Weight: 24 ¹/₃ oz. with 3 fences

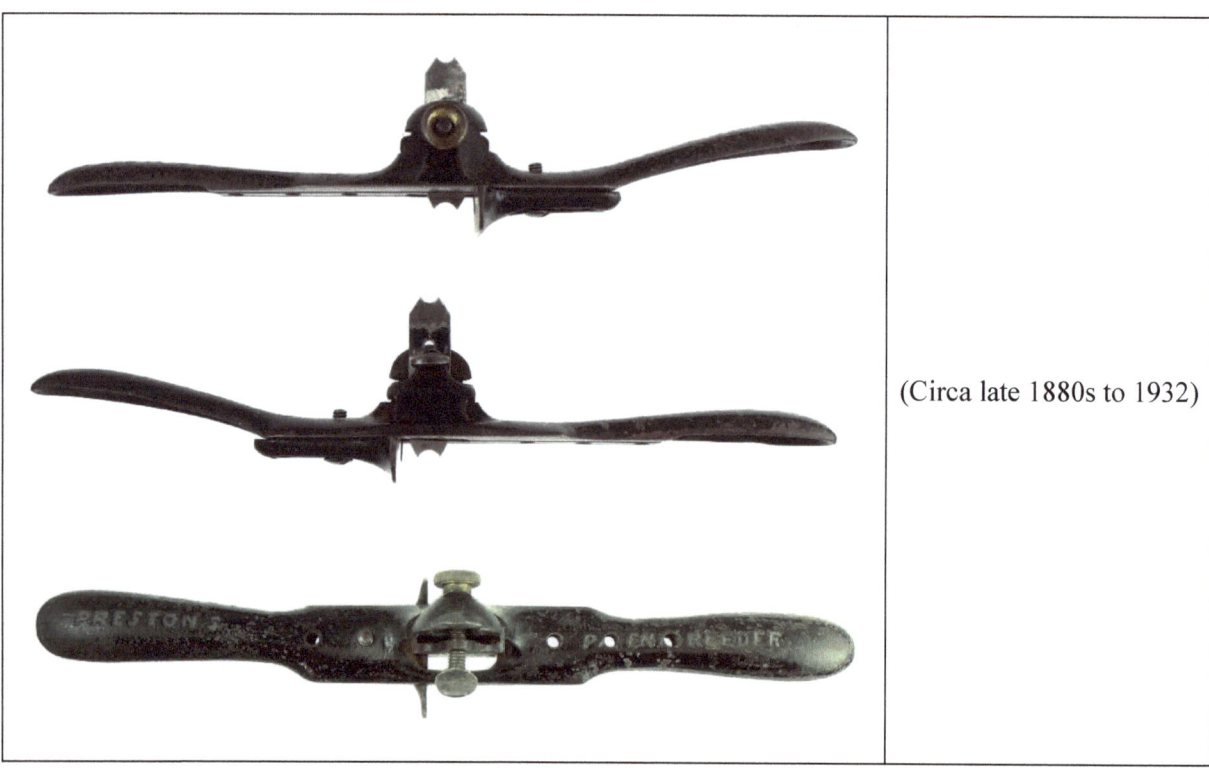

(Circa late 1880s to 1932)

Blades

The 1393 was provided with 7 blades which can easily be reshaped to a custom profile. The 1393 blades did not have the 2 horizontal slots to engage the adjustment nut. 1393P blades can be used in a 1393, but 1393 blades cannot be readily used in a 1393P.

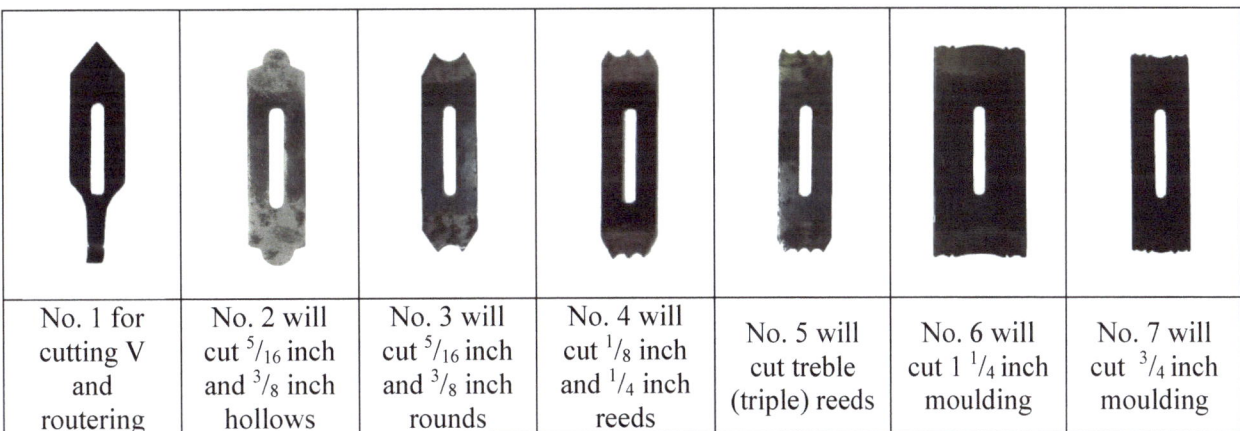

No. 1 for cutting V and routering	No. 2 will cut $5/16$ inch and $3/8$ inch hollows	No. 3 will cut $5/16$ inch and $3/8$ inch rounds	No. 4 will cut $1/8$ inch and $1/4$ inch reeds	No. 5 will cut treble (triple) reeds	No. 6 will cut $1\ 1/4$ inch moulding	No. 7 will cut $3/4$ inch moulding

A set of 1393 blades numbered as in the 1909 catalogue.

Fences

The 1393 and 1393P were supplied with three fences. There is no difference between the fences supplied with the 1393 and 1393P. All three fences are approximately the same size but with different shapes. The fences were straight, convex, and concave.

1393P Patent Adjustable Hand Reeder and Moulding Tool

Description

The lever cap for this tool is covered by patent 8296, issued in 1886. The depth adjuster is covered by patent 12,458, issued in 1885. The No. 1393P was introduced between 1891 and 1895. It appears in the 1895 through 1932 editions of the Preston catalogue. A version with green cellulose paint is suspected, but has never been observed by the author.

Dimensions

Length: 13 ¼ inches
Blade width: ¾ and 1¼ inch wide interchangeable blades
Weight: 20 ⅛ oz. with 1 fence

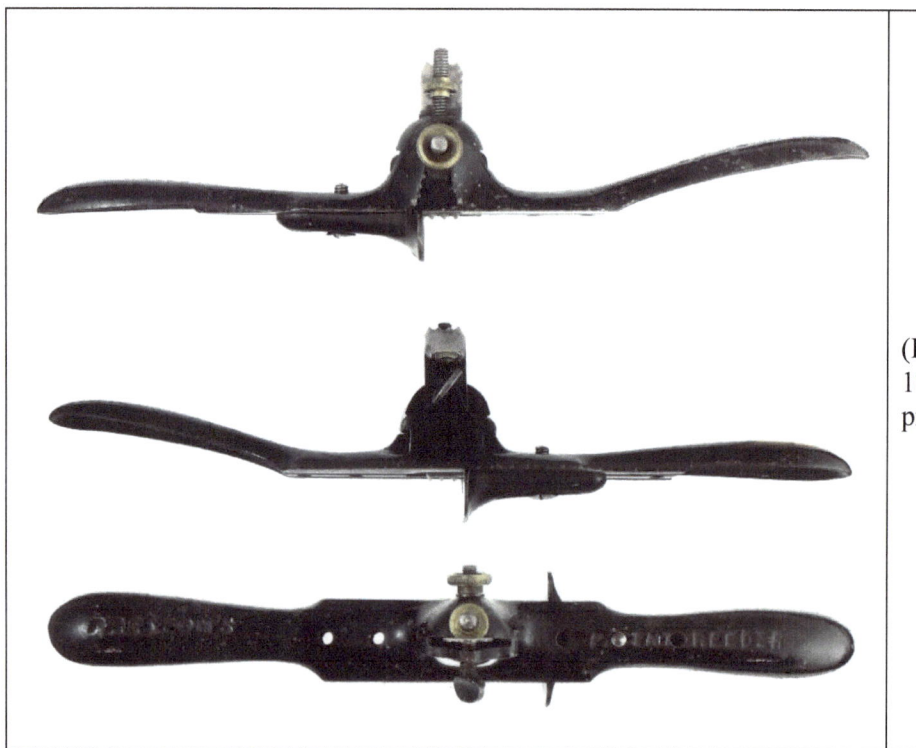

(Introduced between 1891 and 1895. In production until 1932)

Blades

The 1393P was provided with 7 blades which can easily be reshaped to a custom profile. The 1393P blades have the 2 horizontal slots to engage the adjustment nut. 1393P blades can be used in a 1393, but 1393 blades cannot be readily used in a 1393P.

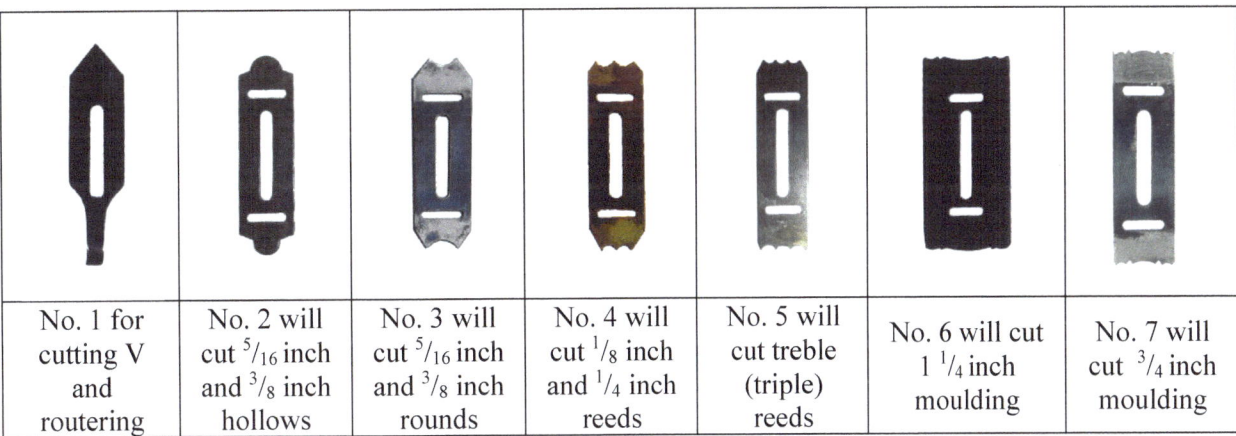

| No. 1 for cutting V and routering | No. 2 will cut $5/16$ inch and $3/8$ inch hollows | No. 3 will cut $5/16$ inch and $3/8$ inch rounds | No. 4 will cut $1/8$ inch and $1/4$ inch reeds | No. 5 will cut treble (triple) reeds | No. 6 will cut $1\ 1/4$ inch moulding | No. 7 will cut $3/4$ inch moulding |

A set of 1393P blades numbered as in the 1909 catalogue.

Fences

The 1393 and 1393P were supplied with three fences. There is no difference between the fences supplied with the 1393 and 1393P. All three fences are approximately the same size but with different shapes. The fences were straight, convex, and concave.

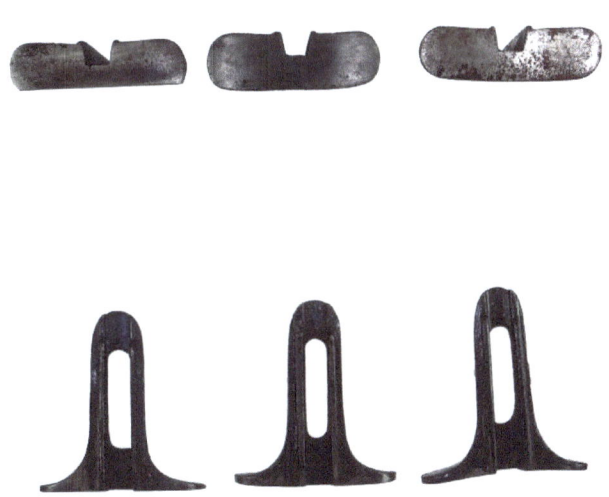

1393S Patent Reeding, Rabbeting, and Moulding tool

Description

This tool is covered by patent 1667, issued in 1888. The 1393S remained in production until Preston ceased trading in 1932. The tool was provided with 6 different cutters. No. 1 cutter is a cutting gauge and grooving tool, No.2 round, No. 3 hollow. Nos. 4 and 5 cutters are adapted for taking out the rabbet of picture frames. No. 5 is also useful for chamfering purposes. No. 6 is for forming mouldings.

Dimensions

Length: $5\,^3/_{16}$ inches
Blade width: Cutting gauge $^3/_{16}$ inch, all others $^9/_{16}$ inch
Weight: $5\,^1/_8$ oz.

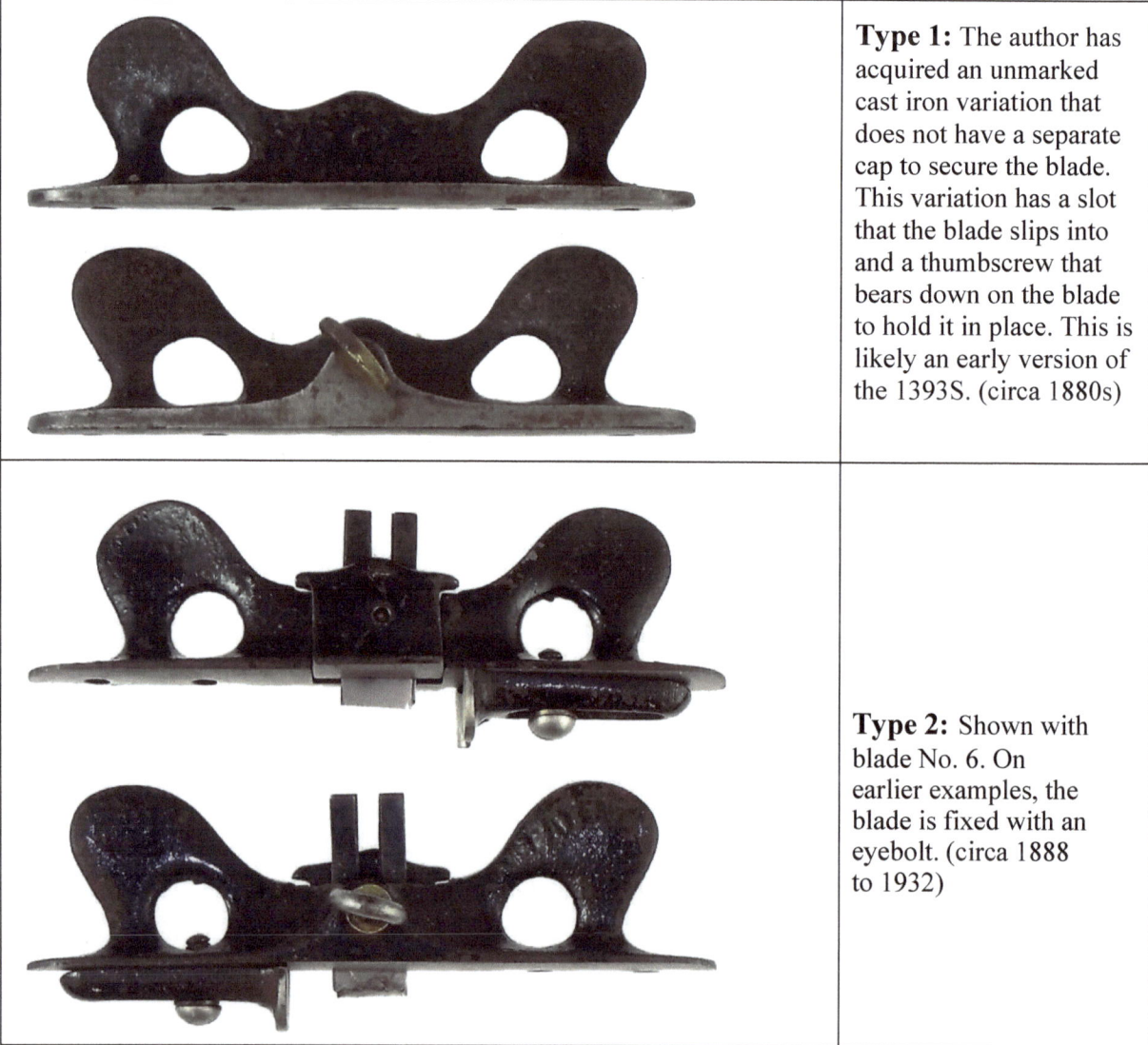

	Type 1: The author has acquired an unmarked cast iron variation that does not have a separate cap to secure the blade. This variation has a slot that the blade slips into and a thumbscrew that bears down on the blade to hold it in place. This is likely an early version of the 1393S. (circa 1880s)
	Type 2: Shown with blade No. 6. On earlier examples, the blade is fixed with an eyebolt. (circa 1888 to 1932)

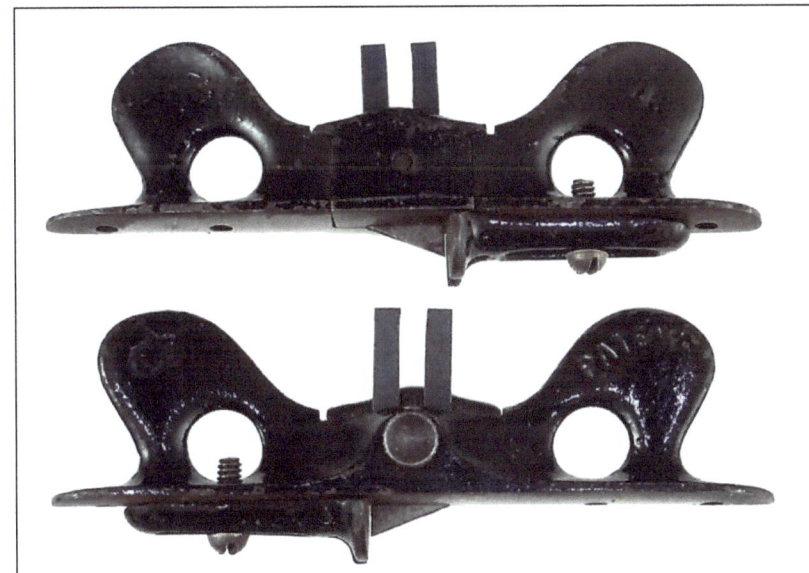

Type 3: Shown with blade No. 5. On later examples, the blade is fixed with a knurled screw (circa 1888 to 1932)

Blades

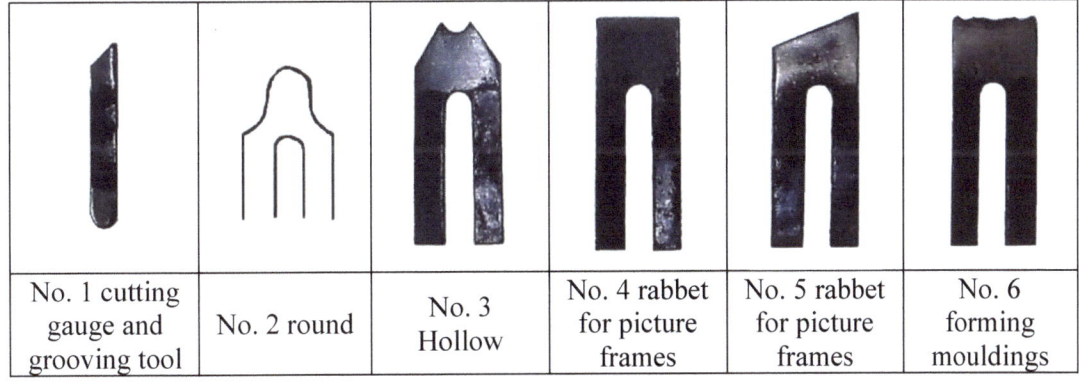

| No. 1 cutting gauge and grooving tool | No. 2 round | No. 3 Hollow | No. 4 rabbet for picture frames | No. 5 rabbet for picture frames | No. 6 forming mouldings |

A set of 1393S blades numbered as in the 1909 catalogue.

1394 Patent Adjustable Circular Quirk or Grooving Router

Description

This tool is held in the upright position when working, presumably for use in places with limited clearance for tool handles. This tool was supplied with 2 fences. The 1394 and 1395 use the same fences. These fences are not interchangeable with any other Preston tools. The 1394 was introduced after 1901, but prior to the publication of the 1909 catalogue. The 1394 was probably discontinued before 1928 as it does not appear in either Price List No. 35 (1928) or Catalogue No. 43 (1932).

Dimensions

Length: 5 $^5/_8$ inches
Blade width: various interchangeable blade widths ($^3/_{32}$ inch to $^3/_{16}$ inch)
Weight: 16 $^7/_8$ oz.

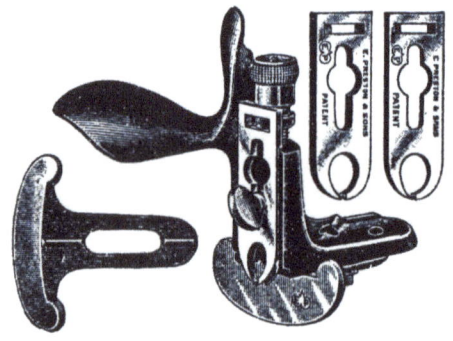

PRESTON PATENT ADJUSTABLE CIRCULAR QUIRK OR GROOVING ROUTER.

This will work exactly as No. 1395 but is different in design.

No. 1394 ... ... 5/- each.

1914 Preston 1394 Catalogue Entry

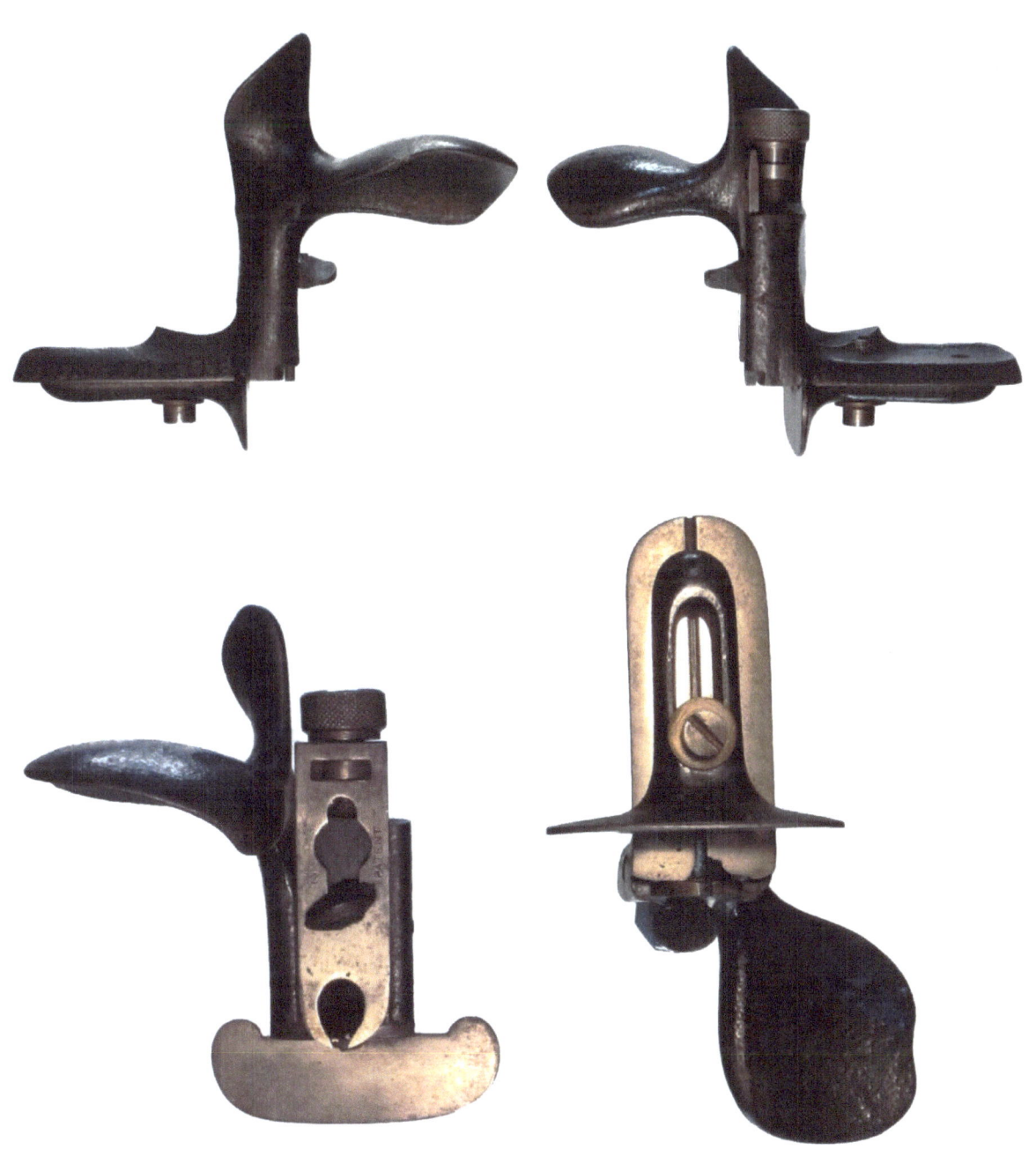

1395 Patent Adjustable Circular Quirk or Grooving Router

Description

This tool is held in the upright position when working, presumably for use in places with limited clearance for tool handles. This tool was supplied with 2 fences. The 1394 and 1395 use the same fences. These fences are not interchangeable with any other Preston tools. The 1395 was introduced after 1901, but prior to the publication of the 1909 catalogue. The 1395 was probably discontinued before 1928 as it does not appear in either Price List No. 35 (1928) or Catalogue No. 43 (1932).

Dimensions

Length: 3 ¼ inches
Blade width: various interchangeable blade widths ($3/32$ inch to $3/16$ inch)
Weight: 15 ¼ oz.

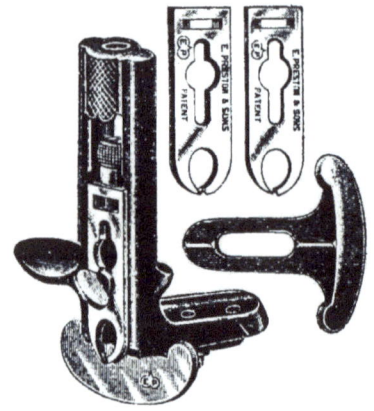

PRESTON PATENT ADJUSTABLE CIRCULAR QUIRK OR GROOVING ROUTER.

This tool is held in an upright position when working and has Adjustable Irons exactly as No. 1388P.

No. 1395 ... ... 5/- each.

1914 Preston No. 1395 catalogue entry

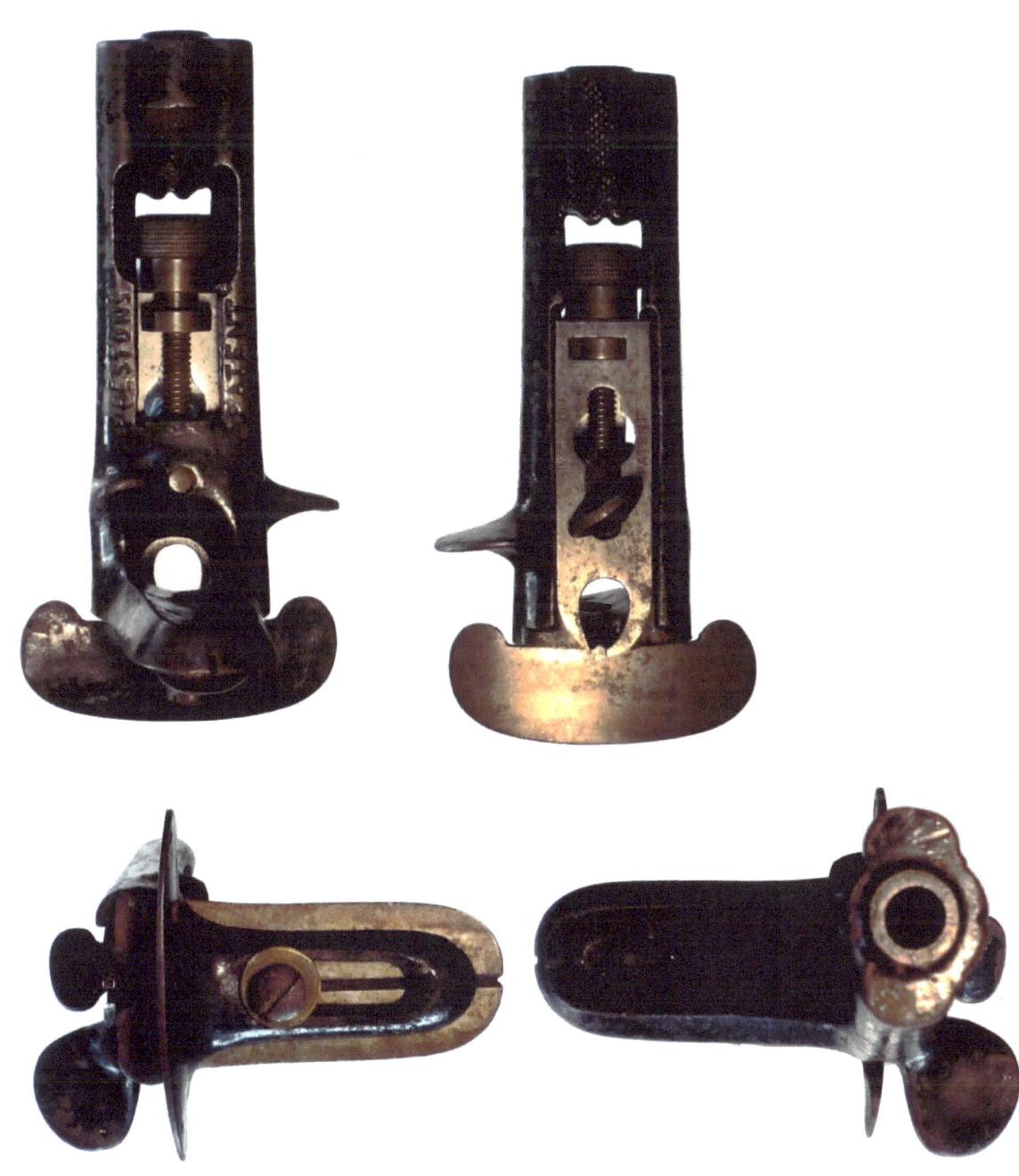

1396 Preston Patent Lining or Stringing Router

Description

The 1396 was not in the 1901 Preston catalogue, but was in the 1909 catalogue. The tool is intended to work as a scratchstock to cut grooves for stringing.

Dimensions

Length: $9\,^7/_8$ inches $10^1/_8$ inches
Blade width: $^1/_{16}$ inches to $^3/_8$ inches
Weight: $14\,^1/_2$ oz.

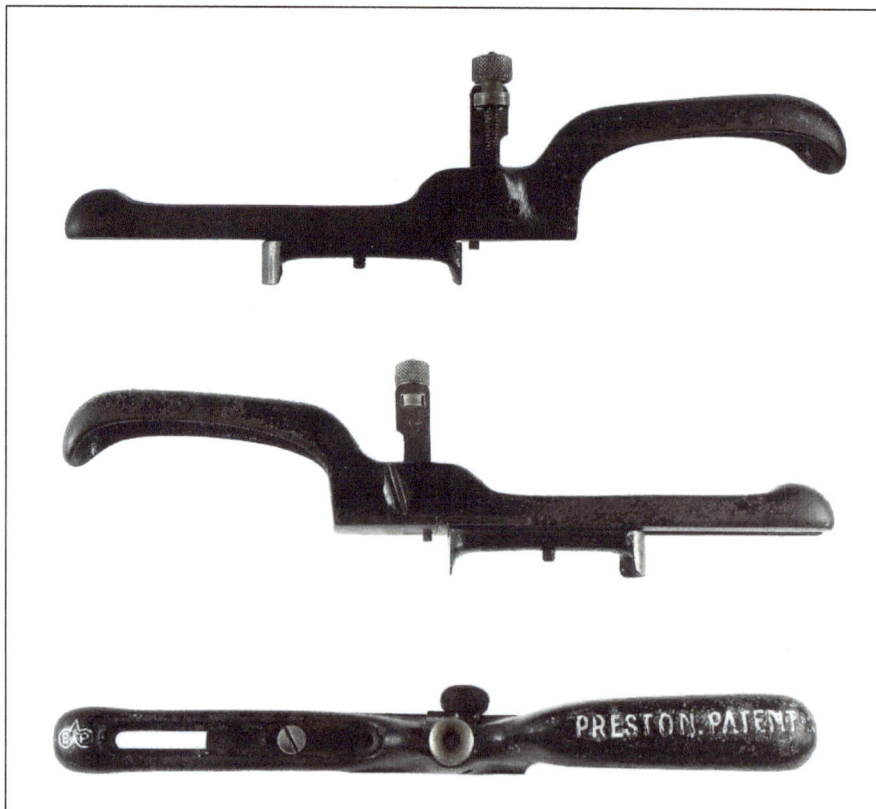

Type 1: Introduced after the 1901 catalogue and prior to 1909. Probably until circa 1912, when the 1398 with the wide fence was introduced. Examples with the Preston Trademark on the lower handle are likely earliest.

Type 2: Introduced after the 1901 catalogue and prior to 1909. Probably until circa 1912, when the 1398 with the wide fence was introduced. Examples with the Preston Trademark on the high handle were likely made later in this time period. All later examples have the trademark on the higher handle.

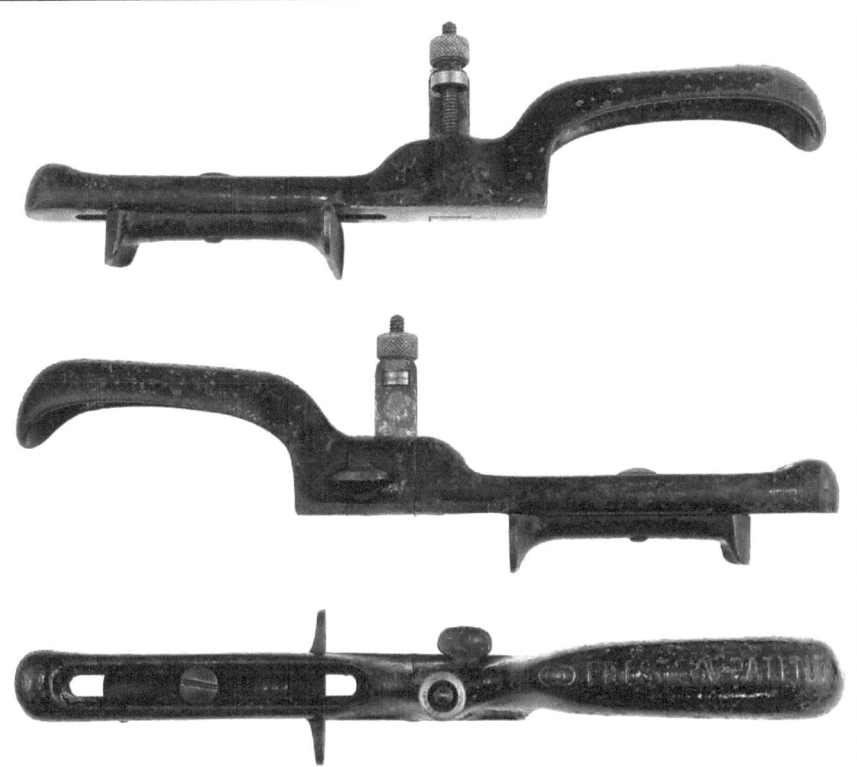

Type 3: (Circa 1912 to late 1920s) Japanned finish with wide fence as seen on 1398

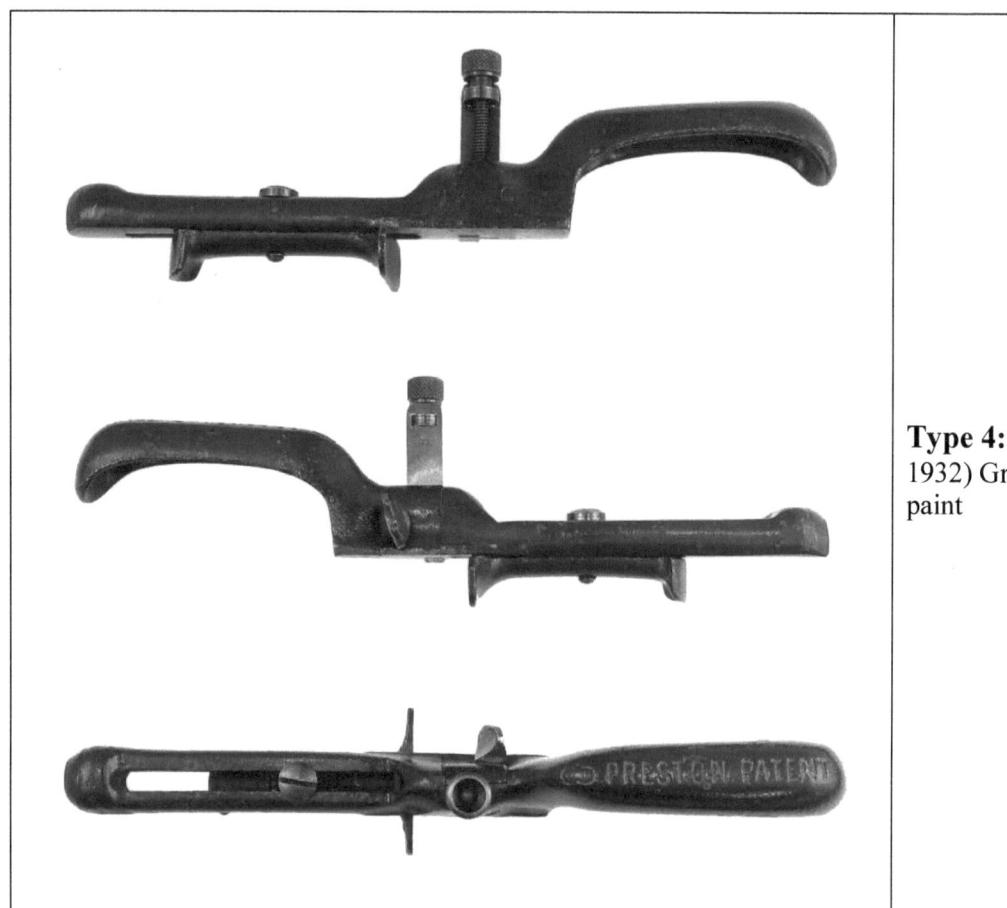

Type 4: (Late 1920s to 1932) Green cellulose paint

Blades

This picture shows the set of 6 blades from $^{1}/_{16}$ inch to $^{3}/_{8}$ inch with a ½ inch blade blank.

1396F Preston Patent Lining or Stringing Router with removable faceplate

Description

The 1396F is a standard 1396 with the addition of a detachable section that supports a second fence. This model is not commonly seen.

Dimensions

Length: 9 ⁷⁄₈ to 10 inches
Blade width: ¹⁄₁₆ inches to ³⁄₈ inches
Weight: 19 ⁷⁄₈ oz.

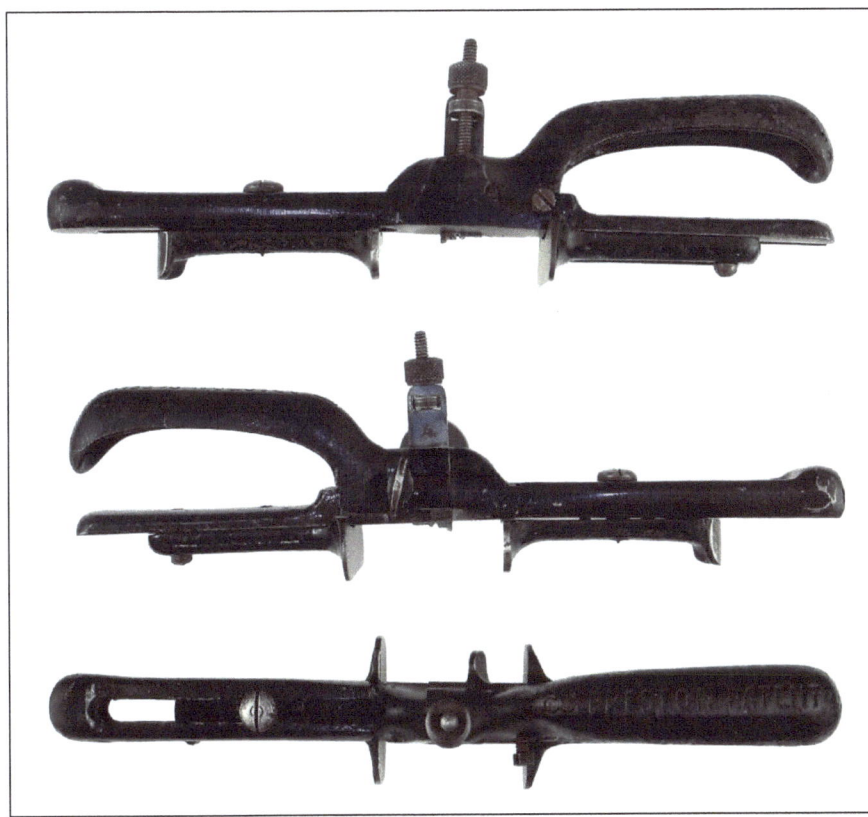

Type 1: 1396F japanned black finish (sometime after 1914 to circa 1930)

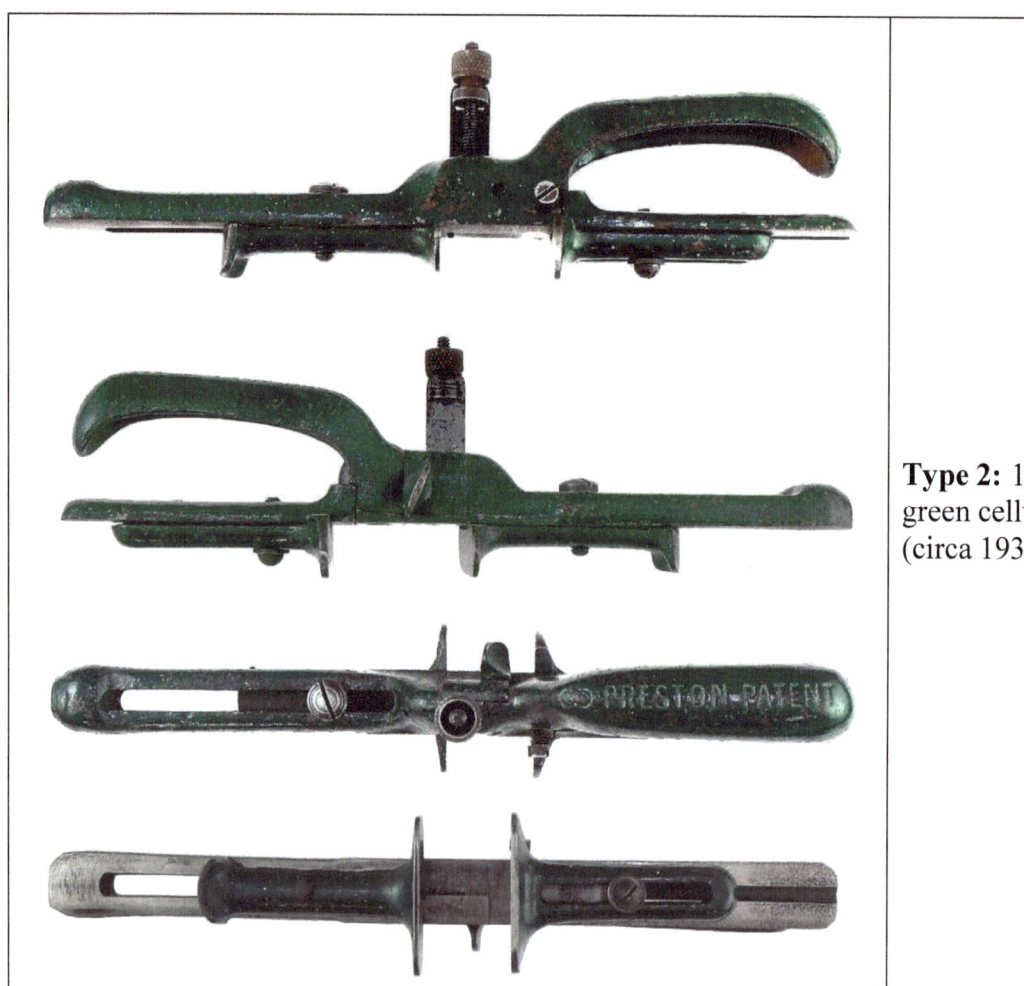

Type 2: 1396F with green cellulose finish (circa 1930 to 1933)

1398 Preston Patent Lining or Stringing Router with round adjustable sliding rod and removable pointed screw pin

Description

The No. 1398 was first listed in *Preston Booklet No. 23* (circa 1911) and then in the *1912 Preston Supplementary and Revised Price List*. The No. 1398 remained in the Preston catalogue until 1932. The fence and the sliding rod cannot be installed at the same time. As such, many examples are found without the sliding rod.

Dimensions

Length: 10 ½ inches (body) the rod is 9 ½ inches long
Blade width: $^{1}/_{16}$ inches to $^{3}/_{8}$ inches
Weight: 17 $^{3}/_{4}$ to 18 $^{1}/_{8}$ oz.

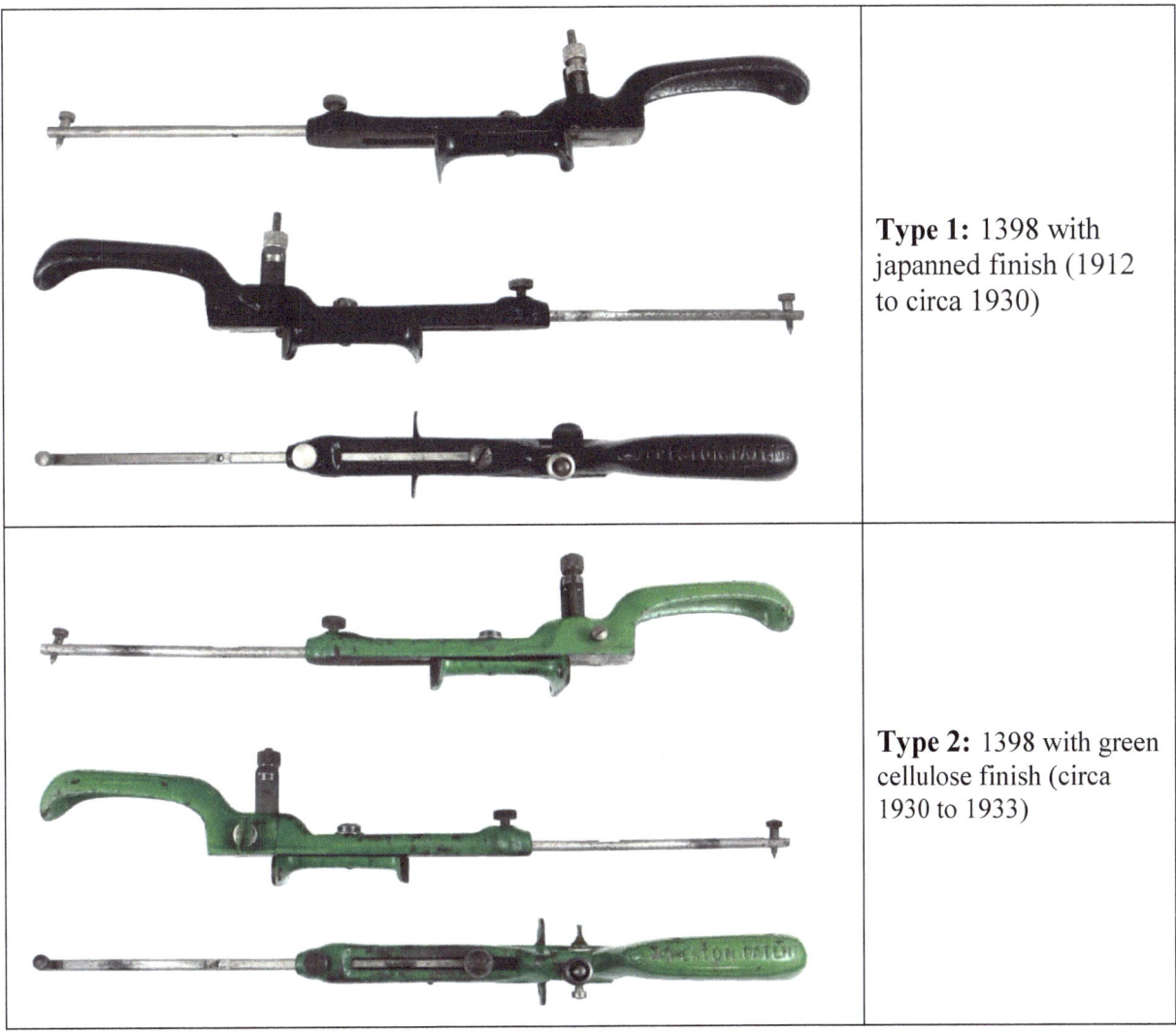

	Type 1: 1398 with japanned finish (1912 to circa 1930)
	Type 2: 1398 with green cellulose finish (circa 1930 to 1933)

2501 Spokeshave with offset handles

Description

This spokeshave is described as model 2501 in the 1914 edition of the Preston catalogue. It is also observed in the catalogues of both George Adams and George Collier, both believed to be from 1912. The 2501 does not appear in either Price List No. 35 (1928) or Catalogue No. 43 (1932). This spokeshave is often incorrectly identified as the 1390H with offset handles.

Dimensions
Length: $10^{1}/_{8}$ inches
Blade width: 2 inches
Weight: $11\ ^{1}/_{2}$ oz.

	2501 with flat face (circa 1914 to 1920s)
	2501 with round face (circa 1914 to 1920s)

2502 Patent Iron Spokeshave

Description

The adjustment mechanism on this spokeshave is covered by patent 20216. The patent was issued in 1912 to Edward Preston and C.E Saunders. Many people incorrectly call this spokeshave a 1391A and believe that it is an early version of Preston's adjustable spokeshave. The model 2502 and model 2503 spokeshaves were catalogued until at least 1928, but were withdrawn prior to 1932.

This spokeshave is described in the 1914 Preston catalogue. The catalogue entry indicates that the depth adjustment was moved to the top plate and the shape of the depth adjustment nut was changed to provide lateral adjustment of the blade. When the thumbscrew securing the blade is loosened, the whole blade and top plate assembly can be rotated, thus providing lateral adjustment. The 2502 spokeshave was japanned.

Dimensions
Length: 10 inches
Blade width: $2^{1}/_{8}$ inches
Weight: $9\,^{3}/_{8}$ oz. to $10\,^{1}/_{3}$ oz.

	2502 flat face (introduced circa 1912 and withdrawn between 1928 and 1932)
	2502 round face (introduced circa 1912 and withdrawn between 1928 and 1932)

2503 Patent Iron Spokeshave

Description

This adjustment mechanism on this spokeshave is covered by patent 20216. The patent was issued in 1912 to Edward Preston and C.E Saunders. Many people incorrectly call this spokeshave a 1391A and believe that it is an early version of Preston's adjustable spokeshave. The model 2502 and model 2503 spokeshaves were catalogued until at least 1928, but were withdrawn prior to 1932.

This spokeshave is described in the 1914 Preston catalogue. The catalogue entry indicates that the depth adjustment was moved to the top plate and the shape of the depth adjustment nut was changed to provide lateral adjustment of the blade. When the thumbscrew securing the blade is loosened, the whole blade and top plate assembly can be rotated, thus providing lateral adjustment. The 2503 spokeshave was nickel plated.

Dimensions
Length: 10 inches
Blade width: $2^1/_8$ inches
Weight: $9\,^3/_8$ oz. to $10\,^1/_3$ oz.

2503 with flat face and wingnut to secure blade (introduced circa 1912 and withdrawn between 1928 and 1932)

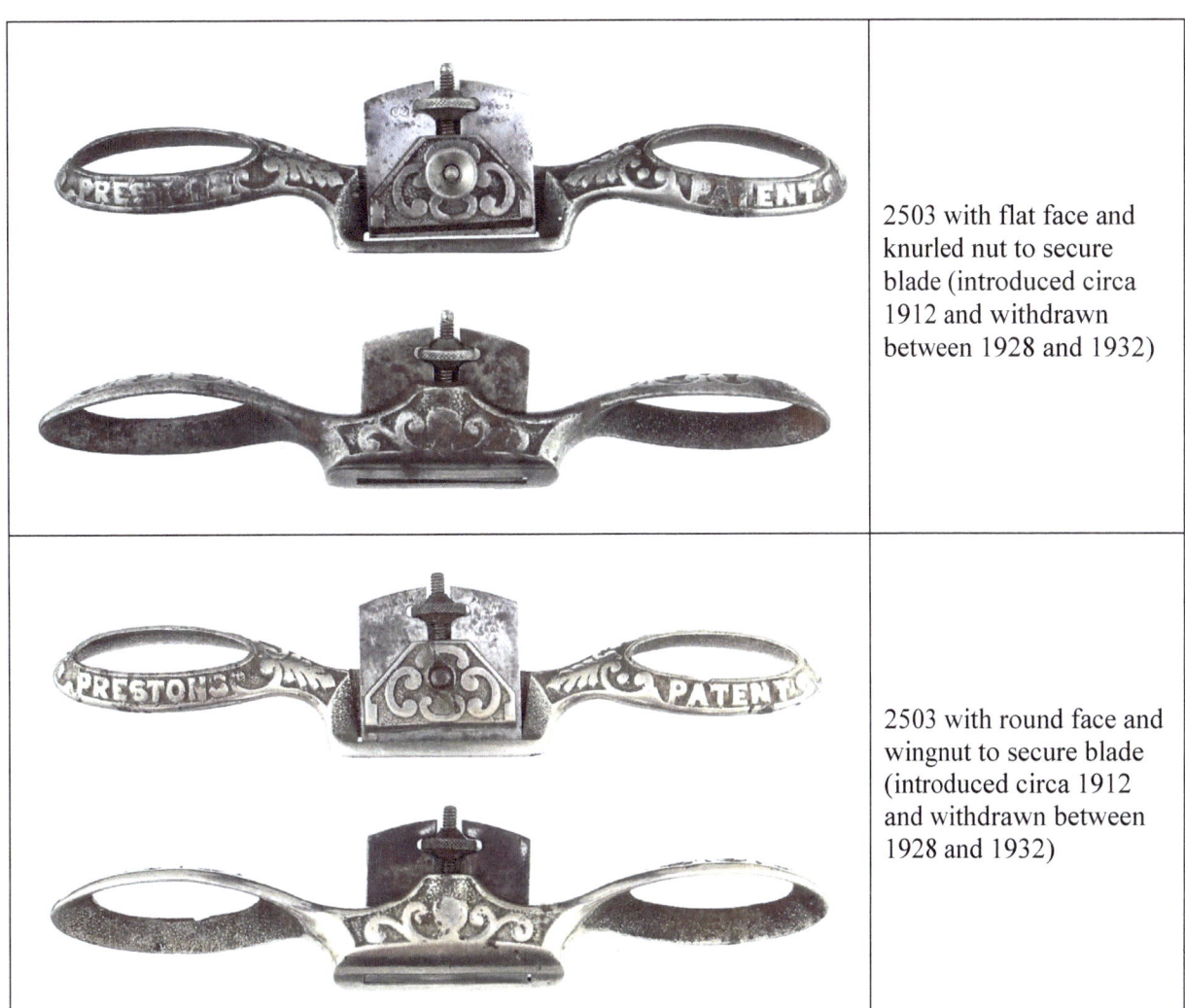

	2503 with flat face and knurled nut to secure blade (introduced circa 1912 and withdrawn between 1928 and 1932)
	2503 with round face and wingnut to secure blade (introduced circa 1912 and withdrawn between 1928 and 1932)

2504 Patent Adjustable Twin Handle, Malleable Iron Rabbeting Shave

Description

The 2504 appears to be similar in design to the Stanley No. 67 universal spokeshave. It was introduced in catalogue No. 26 (1914). It is unknown how long it remained in production, but its rarity would suggest that it was produced in relatively small numbers.

Dimensions

Length: 9 inches
Weight: not available

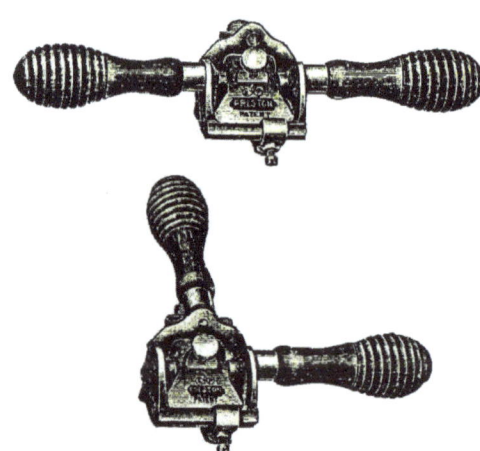

PRESTON PATENT ADJUSTABLE TWIN HANDLE, MALLEABLE IRON RABBETING SHAVE.

Packed one in a Box.

This is a new idea in Rabbeting Shaves and will be found to be a very handy and universal tool.

The Handles are of Rosewood and may be used in positions as shown in drawings. The Shave enables the user to do rabbeting work, or the tool can be used as a Spokeshave. A movable Fence is supplied for width of cut desired.

The Shave is made for straight and circular work. When it is required for circular work the special shaped bottom fitment at back is detached. This fitment although round on its surface really forms and works as a flat face, moving smoothly over the wood in work.

The Cutting Iron is supplied with the PRESTON PATENT ADJUSTMENT and the tool is Nickel Plated.

No. 2504.   Wood Handles, 9 inches, Nickel Plated,
2 inch Cutting Iron   ...   .   **7/6 each.**

1914 Preston No. 2504 Catalogue entry

Charles Parkin & Son's Registered Hand Beader

Description

This stringing router was produced by Charles Parkin & Son, Clarendon Works, Sheffield and has been incorrectly attributed to Preston. It has been documented as a Preston product on page 356 of *Manufactured and Patented Spokeshaves & Similar Tools* by Tom Lammond. The tool does not appear to be rare, but is difficult to find since most sellers cannot identify the manufacturer of this tool. It is marked Rd 181531. The registered design number 181531 was issued on October 26, 1891. Charles Parkin & Son was established in 1860 and remained in business at least until 1913. *White's General and Commercial Directory of Hull, Beverley, Patrington, etc., Seventh Edition, 1882* by William While lists C. Parkin & Son at Clarendon Works, 32, Charlotte Street, Sheffield. *The London Gazette, 4 July 1913* lists Charles Parkin and Son at Clarendon Works, 30 and 32, Charlotte Street, Sheffield. This tool is seen in the 1892 *Melhuish Catalogue no. 6* and the 1899 *Melhuish catalogue no. 11*, but is not seen in the 1912 *Melhuish catalogue No. 21*. Note that these are the consecutive Melhuish woodworking catalogues.

Dimensions

Length: 9 ¼ inches
Blade width: ⅝ inches
Weight: 7 ¼ oz.

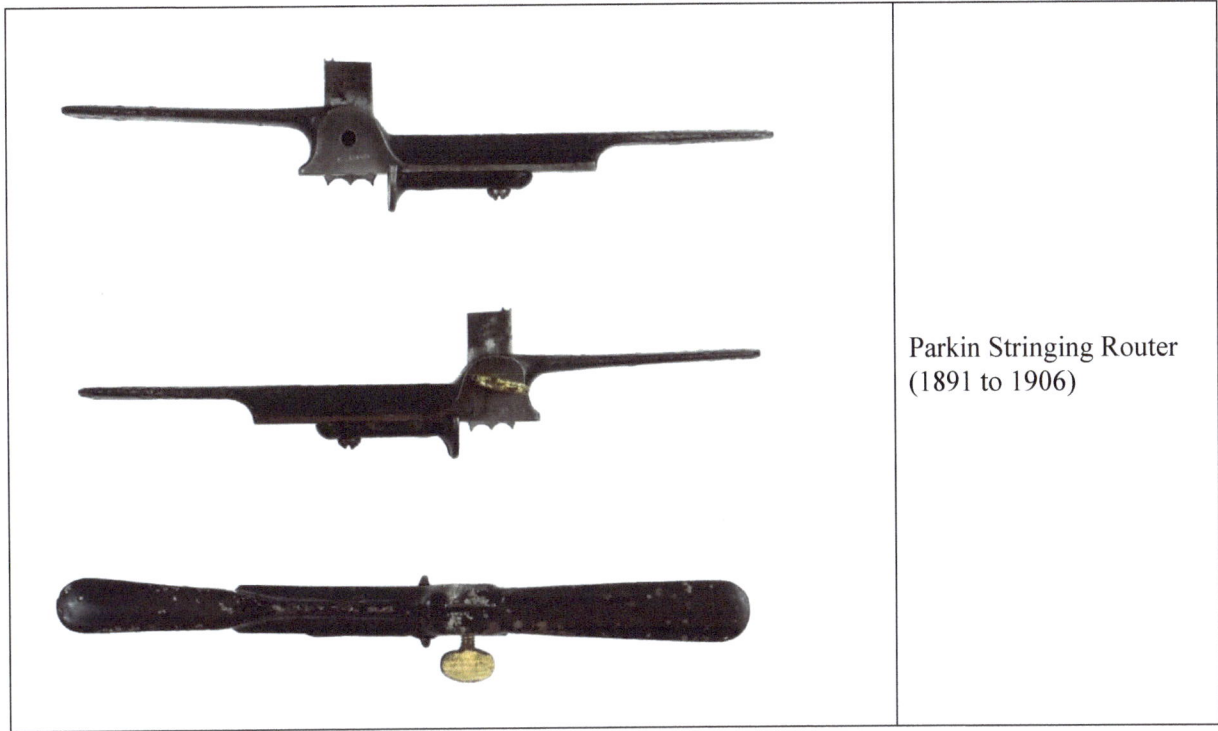

Parkin Stringing Router (1891 to 1906)

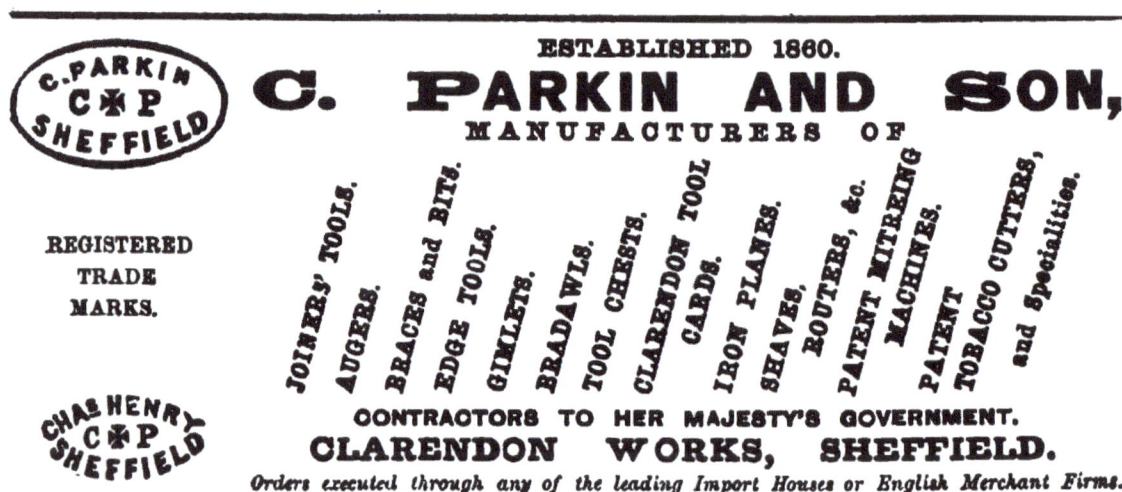

Advertisement in the Australian Handbook (incorporating New Zealand, Fiji, and New Guinea) Shippers, Importers and Professional Directory & Business Guide for 1888

Checklist

✓	Catalogue number	Description
	76	iron spokeshave - japanned black
	76	iron spokeshave - green cellulose
	77	iron spokeshave - japanned black
	77	iron spokeshave - green cellulose
	78	iron spokeshave - japanned black
	78	iron spokeshave - green cellulose
	79	iron spokeshave - japanned black
	79	iron spokeshave - green cellulose
	80	iron spokeshave - japanned black
	80	iron spokeshave – green cellulose
	81	iron spokeshave - japanned black
	81	iron spokeshave - green cellulose
	82	Adjustable mouth iron spokeshave - japanned black
	82	Adjustable mouth iron spokeshave - green cellulose
	83	concave shave similar to 1383 except with chequered handles
	87	iron spokeshave, 2 depth adjustment screws, round face, green cellulose
	88	iron spokeshave, 2 depth adjustment screws, flat face, green cellulose
	89	chamfer spokeshave -green cellulose
	1373	Registered Iron Spokeshave – nickel plated
	1374	Nickel plated top plate
	1374	Nickel plated top plate with red background
	1374P	Registered Iron Spokeshave - round sole, nickel plated, ornate back
	1374P	Registered Iron Spokeshave - flat sole, nickel plated, ornate back
	1374P	Registered Iron Spokeshave - round sole, nickel plated, smooth back
	1377	Round face with ornate back and slotted screw to top plate
	1377	Round face with smooth back and slotted screw to nickel plated top plate
	1377	Flat face with ornate back and nickel plated top plate
	1377	Round face with smooth back and slotted screw to red top plate
	1377T	Embossed back and thumbscrew to top plate
	1377T	Smooth back and thumbscrew to red top plate
	Possible predecessor to No. 78	Iron spokeshave – round face, japanned black

✓	Catalogue number	Description
	1379	iron spokeshave –japanned black
	1380	iron spokeshave - japanned black
	1380 ½	iron spokeshave- flat face, japanned black
	1380 ½	iron spokeshave- round face, japanned black
	1381	iron spokeshave - japanned black
	1381 ½	smooth handles flat face, japanned black
	1381 ½	smooth handles round face, japanned black
	1381 ½	chequered handles flat face, japanned black
	1382	iron spokeshave with adjustable mouth, japanned black
	1382 ½	raised handles , japanned black
	1383	iron spokeshave, concave face, japanned black
	1383 ½	iron spokeshave, convex face, japanned black
	1384	Double cutter iron spokeshave with hollow and flat face, japanned black
	1384	Iron spokeshave with hollow and round face, japanned black
	1385	improved chamfer shave
	1386	improved circular rabbeting and fillister router – japanned black
	1386	improved circular rabbeting and fillister router - green cellulose
	1387A	Oveloe $^3/_8$ inch improved circular sash router
	1387A	Oveloe ½ inch x 1-½ inch improved circular sash router
	1387A	Oveloe $^9/_{16}$ inch x 1-½ inch improved circular sash router
	1387A	Oveloe $^5/_8$ inch x 1-½ inch improved circular sash router
	1387A	Oveloe $^5/_8$ inch x 1¾ inch improved circular sash router
	1387A	Oveloe $^5/_8$ inch x 2 inch improved circular sash router
	1387A	Oveloe $^3/_4$ inch x 1¾ inch improved circular sash router
	1387A	Oveloe $^3/_4$ inch x 2 inch improved circular sash router
	1387B	Lambtongue ½ inch x 1-½ inch improved circular sash router
	1387B	Lambtongue $^9/_{16}$ inch x 1-½ inch improved circular sash router
	1387B	Lambtongue $^5/_8$ inch x 1-½ inch improved circular sash router
	1387B	Lambtongue $^5/_8$ inch x 1¾ inch improved circular sash router
	1387B	Lambtongue $^5/_8$ inch x 2 inch improved circular sash router
	1387B	Lambtongue $^3/_4$ inch x 1¾ inch improved circular sash router
	1387B	Lambtongue $^3/_4$ inch x 2 inch improved circular sash router
	1387C	Gothic ½ inch x 1-½ inch improved circular sash router
	1387C	Gothic $^9/_{16}$ inch x 1-½ inch improved circular sash router
	1387C	Gothic $^5/_8$ inch x 1¾ inch improved circular sash router
	1387C	Gothic $^5/_8$ inch x 2 inch improved circular sash router

✓	Catalogue number	Description
	1387C	Gothic ³/₄ inch x 1¾ inch improved circular sash router
	1387C	Gothic ³/₄ inch x 2 inch improved circular sash router
	1387D	¼ inch improved circular common oveloe router
	1387D	³/₈ inch improved circular common oveloe router
	1387D	½ inch improved circular common oveloe router
	1387D	⁵/₈ inch improved circular common oveloe router
	1387D	³/₄ inch improved circular common oveloe router
	1387E	¼ x ¼ inch improved circular equal or square oveloe router
	1387E	³/₈ x ³/₈ inch improved circular equal or square oveloe router
	1387E	½ x ½ inch improved circular equal or square oveloe router
	1387E	⁹/₁₆ x ⁹/₁₆ inch improved circular equal or square oveloe router
	1387E	⁵/₈ x ⁵/₈ inch improved circular equal or square oveloe router
	1387E	¾ x ¾ inch improved circular equal or square oveloe router
	1388	Improved Circular Quirk or Grooving Router – japanned black
	1388	Improved Circular Quirk or Grooving Router - green cellulose
	1388P	Patent Adjustable Circular Quirk or Grooving Router – japanned black
	1388P	Patent Adjustable Circular Quirk or Grooving Router - green cellulose
	1389	⅛ inch circular bead router
	1389	³/₁₆ inch circular bead router
	1389	¼ inch circular bead router
	1389	⁵/₁₆ inch circular bead router
	1389	³/₈ inch circular bead router
	1389	⁷/₁₆ inch circular bead router
	1389	½ inch circular bead router
	1389	⁹/₁₆ inch circular bead router
	1389	⁵/₈ inch circular bead router
	1389	¾ inch circular bead router
	1389	⁷/₈ inch circular bead router
	1389	1 inch circular bead router
	1390	Type 1 with straight handles, flat face
	1390	Type 1 with straight handles, round face
	1390	Type 1 - flat face smooth top plate, rectangular adjustment notch in blade, narrow knurled section on adjustment nut
	1390	Type 1 - round face smooth top plate, rectangular adjustment notch in blade, narrow knurled section on adjustment nut
	1390	Type 2 - flat face smooth top plate, curved adjustment notch in blade, wide knurled section on adjustment nut

✓	Catalogue number	Description
	1390	Type 2 – round face smooth top plate, curved adjustment notch in blade, wide knurled section on adjustment nut
	1390	Type 3 - flat face chequered top plate
	1390	Type 3 - round face chequered top plate
	1390	Type 4 - flat face ornate top plate
	1390	Type 4 - round face ornate top plate
	1390H	Type 1 - Japanned, flat face, no lateral adjuster, smooth top plate, rectangular adjustment notch in blade, narrow knurled section on adjustment nut
	1390H	Type 1 - Japanned, round face, no lateral adjuster, smooth top plate, rectangular adjustment notch in blade, narrow knurled section on adjustment nut
	1390H	Type 2 - Japanned, flat face, no lateral adjuster, smooth top plate, curved adjustment notch in blade, wide knurled section on adjustment nut
	1390H	Type 2 - Japanned, round face, no lateral adjuster, smooth top plate, curved adjustment notch in blade, wide knurled section on adjustment nut
	1390H	Type 3 - Japanned, flat face, no lateral adjuster, chequered top plate
	1390H	Type 3 - Japanned, round face, no lateral adjuster, chequered top plate
	1390H	Type 4 - Japanned, flat face, no lateral adjuster, ornate top plate
	1390H	Type 4 - Japanned, round face, no lateral adjuster, ornate top plate
	1390H	Type 5 - Japanned, flat face, lateral adjuster, ornate top plate
	1390H	Type 5 - Japanned, round face, lateral adjuster, ornate top plate
	1390H	Type 6 - 1391 casting, Japanned, flat face, lateral adjuster, marked "PRESTONS PATENT"
	1390H	Type 6 - 1391 casting, Japanned, round face, lateral adjuster, marked "PRESTONS PATENT"
✓	1390H	Type 7 - 1391 casting, Japanned, flat face, lateral adjuster, red background on top plate, marked "PRESTONS PATENT"
	1390H	Type 7 - 1391 casting Japanned, round face, lateral adjuster, red background on top plate, marked "PRESTONS PATENT"
	1390H	Type 8 - 1391 casting, Japanned, flat face, lateral adjuster, red background on top plate, marked "PRESTON. ENG."
	1390H	Type 8 - 1391 casting, Japanned, round face, lateral adjuster, red background on top plate, marked "PRESTON. ENG."
	1390H	Type 9 - 1391 casting, green cellulose, flat face, lateral adjuster, marked "PRESTON. ENG."
	1390H	Type 9- 1391 casting, green cellulose, round face, lateral adjuster, marked "PRESTON. ENG."
	1391	Type 1 - Nickel plated, flat face, no lateral adjuster, rectangular adjustment notch in blade, narrow knurled section on adjustment nut, marked "PRESTONS PATENT"

✓	Catalogue number	Description
	1391	Type 1 - Nickel plated, round face, no lateral adjuster, rectangular adjustment notch in blade, narrow knurled section on adjustment nut, marked "PRESTONS PATENT"
	1391	Type 2 - Nickel plated, flat face, no lateral adjuster, curved adjustment notch in blade, wide knurled section on adjustment nut, marked "PRESTONS PATENT"
	1391	Type 2 - Nickel plated, round face, no lateral adjuster, curved adjustment notch in blade, wide knurled section on adjustment nut, marked "PRESTONS PATENT"
	1391	Type 3 - Nickel plated, flat face, lateral adjuster, marked " PRESTONS PATENT"
	1391	Type 3 -Nickel plated, round face, lateral adjuster, marked "PRESTONS PATENT"
	1391	Type 4 - Nickel plated, flat faced, lateral adjuster, marked "PRESTON. ENG."
	1391	Type 4 - Nickel plated, round faced, lateral adjuster, marked "PRESTON. ENG."
	1392	Type 1 -Smooth top plate, short fences, tapered adjustment nut
	1392	Type 2 -Smooth top plate, long fences
	1392	Type 3 - chequered top plate, no lateral adjuster
	1392	Type 4 - chequered top plate with lateral adjuster
	1393	Patent Hand Reeder and Moulding Tool
	1393P	Patent Adjustable Hand Reeder and Moulding Tool
	1393S solid body	like 1393S except not marked patent and made with solid body
	1393S	Patent Reeding, Rabbeting, and Moulding tool, loop blade retaining nut
	1393S	Patent Reeding, Rabbeting, and Moulding tool, knurled blade retaining nut
	1394	Patent Adjustable Circular Quirk or Grooving Router
	1395	Patent Adjustable Circular Quirk or Grooving Router
	1396	Preston Patent Lining or Stringing Router, narrow fence, EP trademark on low handle, japanned black
	1396	Preston Patent Lining or Stringing Router, narrow fence, , EP trademark on high handle, japanned black
	1396	Preston Patent Lining or Stringing Router, wide fence, japanned black
	1396	Preston Patent Lining or Stringing Router, wide fence, green cellulose
	1396F	Preston Patent Lining or Stringing Router with removable faceplate – japanned black
	1396F	Preston Patent Lining or Stringing Router with removable faceplate - green cellulose
	1398	Preston Patent Lining or Stringing Router with round adjustable sliding rod and removable pointed screw pin – japanned black
	1398	Preston Patent Lining or Stringing Router with round adjustable sliding rod and removable pointed screw pin - green cellulose

✓	Catalogue number	Description
	2501	Japanned, flat face, lateral adjuster, ornate top plate, offset handles
	2501	Japanned, round face, lateral adjuster, ornate top plate, offset handles
	2502	Japanned, flat face, blade adjuster in top plate
	2502 R.F	Japanned, round face, blade adjuster in top plate
	2503	Nickel plated, flat face, blade adjuster in top plate
	2503 R.F.	Nickel plated, round face, blade adjuster in top plate
	2504	Patent Adjustable Twin Handle, Malleable Iron Rabbeting Shave (similar to Stanley 67)

Listing of Catalogues and Other Ephemera

The catalogues, booklets, and price lists published by Edward Preston were numbered sequentially from 1 to 43. This sequence included several page revised price lists to full line catalogues. Revised Price List No. 35 applies to catalogues Nos. 26 and 26R. This would indicate that no new full line catalogues were published between 1914 and 1928. In this time period, there would have been booklets and revised price sheets. Catalogue No. 26R is believed to be a small format edition of Catalogue No. 26. The small format might be the result of shortages during and just after the First World War. Catalogue No. 26 was printed with colour illustrations while No. 26R was printed in black and white. The example of catalogue No. 26R available to the author had additional pages inserted when it was bound. The inserted pages are numbered with an "a" after the page number, e.g. page 4a is inserted adjacent to page 4.

Catalogue number	Date	Publication Type	Description
4	August 1891	catalogue	1891 full line catalogue
5	July 1895	catalogue	1895 full line catalogue
6	July 1901	catalogue	1901 full line catalogue
18	May 1909	catalogue	1909 full line catalogue. 168 pages
20	July 1, 1910	price correction sheets	4 pages of addendums, price corrections, and new tools
23	undated, circa 1911	booklet	95 page booklet. (4 $^3/_4$ inches x 6 $^1/_2$ inches)
25	July 1, 1912	Supplementary and revised price list	12 page supplement
26	May 1914	catalogue	1914 full line catalogue. 188 pages.
26R	unknown	catalogue	Small format edition of catalogue No. 26 (5 $^3/_4$ inches x 7 $^1/_4$ inches)
27	unknown	catalogue	91 pages. (11 ½ inches x 9 inches)
31B	July 1927	Revised and Reduced Prices and Terms	6 page supplement that applies to catalogues 26 and 26R.
35	February 1928	Revised and Reduced Prices and Terms	6 page supplement to catalogues Nos. 26 and 26R.
43	October 1932	catalogue	1932 full line catalogue - last before selling to Rabone
Rabone No. 27	1933	catalogue	11 pages addendum indicating Edward Preston & Sons has been incorporated in John Rabone & Sons

According to "Printing During the First World War", dated 14th September 2015, retrieved from http://www.typographichub.org/articles/entry/printing-in-the-first-world-war/ on March 20, 2018, many publications were suspended and the book trade was halted. The 1921 International Printing Machinery and Allied Trades Exhibition (IPEX) marked the return to normalcy in the British printing industry. As a result, there were very few tool catalogues published once the First World War began until the 1920s.

References

Lamond, Thomas, *Manufactured and Patented Spokeshaves & Similar Tools*, 1997

Melhuish, Richard Ltd., *Woodworkers' Tools and Machines Catalogue*, London, England, 1885

Melhuish, Richard Ltd., *Woodworkers' Tools and Machines Catalogue No. 6*, London, England, 1892

Melhuish, Richard Ltd., *Woodworkers' Tools and Machines Catalogue No. 10*, London, England, 1899

Melhuish, Richard Ltd., *Woodworkers' Tools and Machines Catalogue No. 21*, London, England, 1912

Melhuish, Richard Ltd., *Woodworkers' Tools and Machines Catalogue No. 25*, London, England, 1925

Murland, Tony, *Murlands Antique Tool Value Guide 2007/08*

Nurse, Charles & Co., *The "Invicta" Illustrated Price List of Mechanics' Tools & Machinery, No. 12*, London, England, Autumn 1902

Nurse, Charles & Co., *The "Invicta" Illustrated Price List of Mechanics' Tools & Machinery, No. 14*, London, England, circa 1908

Nurse, Charles & Co., The "Invicta" Illustrated Price List of Mechanics' Tools & Machinery, No. 16, London, England, June 1914

Nurse, Charles & Co., *The "Invicta" Illustrated Price List of Mechanics' Tools & Machinery, No. 23*, London, England, undated, but after 1919

Nurse, Charles & Co., The *"Invicta" Illustrated Price List of Mechanics' Tools & Machinery, No. 25*, undated

Nurse, Charles & Co., *The "Invicta" Illustrated Price List of Mechanics' Tools & Machinery, No. 28*, London, England, circa 1926

Preston, Edward & Sons, *Illustrated Price List of Boxwood, Ivory, Brass & Steel Rules, Planes, Spirit Levels, Carpenters & Joiners' Improved Tools &c., 4th Ed.*, Birmingham, England, August, 1891

Preston, Edward & Sons, *Illustrated Price List of Boxwood, Ivory, Brass & Steel Rules, Planes, Spirit Levels, Carpenters & Joiners' Improved Tools &c., 5th Ed.*, Birmingham, England, July 31, 1895

Preston, Edward & Sons, Ltd., *Illustrated Price List of Rules, Spirit Levels, Planes and Tools &c., 6th Ed.*: 1901, Birmingham, England Reprint: K. Roberts Pub. Co. 1979

Preston, Edward & Sons, Ltd., *Illustrated Catalogue of Rules, Levels, Plumbs & Levels, Thermometers, Planes, Improved Woodworker's and Mechanics' Tools &c.*, Catalogue No. 18: May 1909, Birmingham, England Reprint: Astragal Press 1991

Preston, Edward & Sons, Ltd., *Rules, Measures, Levels, Plumbs and Levels, Planes, Mechanics' Tools, Booklet No. 23*, Birmingham, England, circa 1911

Preston, Edward & Sons, Ltd., *Supplementary and Revised Price List of Boxwood, Ivory, Brass Rules, Tailors' Squares, Shoemakers' Size Sticks, Contraction Laths, Parallel Rules, height Standards, Boat Levels, Spirit Levels, and New Patterns of Plumbs and Levels, Trammel Heads, Plumb Bobs, Iron Planes, Grooving Routers, and Depthing Squares, List No. 25*: July 1, 1912, Birmingham, England Reprint: Astragal Press 1991

Preston, Edward & Sons, Ltd., *Illustrated Catalogue of Rules, Levels, Plumbs & Levels, Thermometers, Measuring Tapes, Planes, Improved Woodworkers' and Mechanics' Tools &c., Catalogue No. 26*: May 1914, Birmingham, England

Preston, Edward & Sons, Ltd., *Revised and Reduced Prices and Terms for Trammel Heads, Plumb Bobs, Iron Planes, Iron Spokeshaves, Reeders, routers, Mitre Boxes, Shuteing Boards, Steel Squares, &c., List No. 35*: February 1928, Birmingham, England

Preston, Edward & Sons, Ltd., *Illustrated Catalogue of Rules, Levels, Plumbs & Levels, Thermometers, Measuring Tapes, Planes, Improved Woodworkers' and Mechanics' Tools &c., Catalogue No. 43*: October 1932, Birmingham, England

Rabone, John &Sons Ltd., *John Rabone & Sons Ltd. Incorporating Edward Preston & Sons Ltd., Catalogue No. 27*, 1933, Birmingham, England

Tyzack, S & Son Ltd., *Tools and Machines for Wood and Metal Workers, Cat. No. 625*, London, England, undated, circa 1925.

Tyzack, S & Son Ltd., *Tools and Machines for Wood and Metal Workers, Cat. No. 630*, London, England, undated, circa 1930.

Tyzack, S & Son Ltd., *Tools and Machines for Wood and Metal Workers, Cat. No. 640*, London, England, undated, circa 1940.